Five Shires by Ra

Conten

OTHER BOOKS IN THE SAME SERIES AS THIS ONE are obtainable from the Railway Development Society Sales Officer, Mr G. Kent, 35A Clarendon Road, Luton, Beds. LU2 7PQ – or from any bookshop:

EAST ANGLIA BY RAIL	ISBN 0 7117 0192 X
LINCOLNSHIRE BY RAIL	ISBN 0 9510221 0 5
MIDLANDS BY RAIL	ISBN 0 9510450 0 8
NORTH EAST BY RAIL	ISBN 0 9511188 0 3
CHESHIRE AND NORTH WALES BY RAIL	ISBN 0 9511189 0 0
KENT AND EAST SUSSEX BY RAIL	ISBN 0 9511192 0 6

NB *East Anglia by Rail* is published by Jarrolds; the other books are published by the Railway Development Society's relevant Branches.

The Railway Passenger Services Of The Five Shires

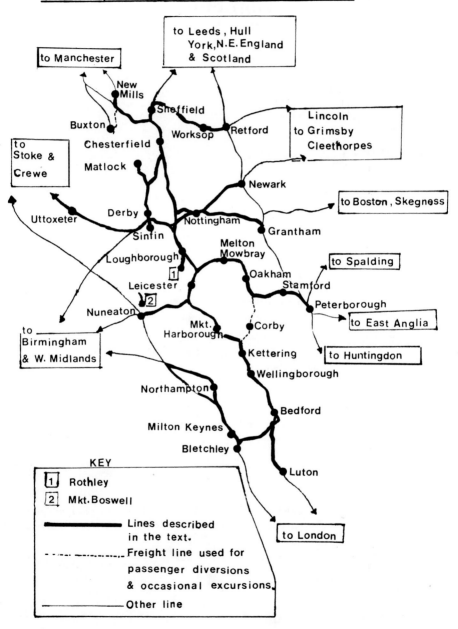

to Leeds, Hull York, N.E. England & Scotland

to Manchester

New Mills

to Stoke & Crewe

Buxton

Sheffield

Chesterfield

Worksop

Retford

Lincoln to Grimsby Cleethorpes

Matlock

Newark

to Boston, Skegness

Uttoxeter

Derby

Nottingham

Grantham

Sinfin

Melton Mowbray

to Spalding

Loughborough

Oakham

Stamford

1 Leicester

Peterborough

2

to East Anglia

Nuneaton

Mkt. Harborough

Corby

to Huntingdon

to Birmingham & W. Midlands

Kettering

Wellingborough

Northampton

Bedford

Milton Keynes

Bletchley

Luton

to London

KEY

1 Rothley
2 Mkt. Boswell

—— Lines described in the text.

-·-·-·-·-·- Freight line used for passenger diversions & occasional excursions.

——— Other line

Five Shires by Rail

Introduction

350 miles of rail line thread their way around these rolling English shires.

75 British Rail stations let the visitor alight and tackle the Pennine Way at Edale; shop in ultra-modern Milton Keynes; take a steam trip into the past at Loughborough; sail 750 feet up in a cable car at Matlock Bath; eat the renowned pork pies of Melton Mowbray; seek entertainment, interest or relaxation in lively cities, market towns and peaceful villages.

The varied scenery observed from the train window ranges from the steep northern slopes of the Chilterns to the rocky Peak District of Derbyshire; from flat rich farmland in the Vale of Belvoir to the unique crooked spire of Chesterfield, with the hunting shires of Northamptonshire and Leicestershire in between.

The trains also vary – from modern electrics in Bedfordshire to smart diesel 'Sprinters' in Nottinghamshire; from vintage steam trains on preserved lines in Leicestershire to High Speed Trains running at up to 125 mph on the Midland Main Line.

That Main Line is the backbone of these five counties' rail system, linking them with London's palatial St. Pancras terminus and bringing, for example, Leicester – 99 miles from the capital – to within just 83 minutes from it by the fastest trains. There are also direct Inter-City services from major population centres of the West Midlands, Yorkshire, the North East and, increasingly, the North West; while through trains also run from Humberside, Lincolnshire and East Anglia.

There are many opportunities for day trips in these five shires. Indeed, what was probably the first ever rail excursion was organised in this area from Leicester to Loughborough in 1841 by a man called Thomas Cook, who went on to develop one of the world's most famous travel companies.

So whether your interest is in energetic open-air pursuits or shopping and entertainment in modern cities; delving into industrial archaeology or watching and participating in sport; roving the rails or surveying the scenery – there is something for you in these five shires of East and North Midlands.

Of course, the region once had more lines and stations than today, as did all other parts of Great Britain, before the closures of the 1950s and 1960s. But since then, four stations have reopened, five completely new ones have been built, and short sections of line have been reopened to passengers by British Rail or preservation societies. Campaigns are under way for more reopenings and more electrification – and the more the network is used, the greater the chances of further improvement and expansion.

4

Class 317 'Bed-Pan' electric multiple unit on local service to Bedford. (*Photo* John C. Baker.)

KEY TO LINE DIAGRAMS

LUTON Staffed station; booking office; train information available. Seats and shelter at station.

Bingham Unstaffed station – pay on the train.

Hull Continuous line – through trains, here shown running to the station named from the line on the diagram.
Dashed line – connecting rail service.

Station and broken line – shown for reference only. Intermediate stations and connections not shown.

ROTHLEY Preserved station.

B'ham – Birmingham
L Eu – London Euston
L St P – London St Pancras
M Pic – Manchester Piccadilly
Nott'm – Nottingham

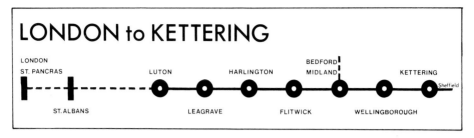

LONDON to KETTERING

MIDLAND MAIN LINE
LONDON (St. Pancras) – LUTON –
BEDFORD – KETTERING

by Bob Mullins and Pete Gerrard

Welcome to the Midland! Under William Barlow's magnificent 1870s curved roof stand High Speed Trains and new 'Bed-Pan' electric units waiting to take the traveller up this historic line to places as diverse as Flitwick and Sheffield.

The passage through the North London suburbs of Hendon, Mill Hill, Elstree and Radlett on an H.S.T. or an electric unit on a fast service can be exhilarating as they tackle the many adverse gradients with ease. It seems that no sooner has St. Albans City curve been negotiated that the town of Luton appears on the horizon.

Luton, (pop. 166,000) which is famous for hat making and Vauxhall cars, stretches out away from the station with the Museum and Art Gallery quite near the Old Bedford Road. The museum has a large collection of pillow lace along with an interesting selection of archaeological and natural history items from South Bedfordshire. There is also an Audio Visual projection unit relating the story of the Luton hat industry which was derived from the ability of the local farming families to plait straw. Modern day needs are also catered for with one of the largest covered shopping centres in the country – The Arndale – only a few minutes walk from the station. Next to the centre is the Tourist Information office on whose outside wall is a large, well-painted mural.

For food and drink the *Vine Inn*, just off the A6 outside the main shopping area in Castle Street, offers good bar food with Greene King IPA and Abbot real ale and Stones, Tartan, Harp and Fosters on pressure.

The bus station, which is situated next to the railway station, is ideal if the visitor wants to see outlying parts of Luton, such as the famous airport which now has a new service called 'The Luton Flyer' with a train departing every half hour from St. Pancras during the day and every hour during the night (24.00 to 05.00). Each of the trains runs fast, with only two stops, before Luton is reached, and connects with a waiting coach for the eight minute trip to the airport.

The bus station can also be handy for visiting such places as Luton Hoo, two miles south of the town. This mansion dating from 1767 contains the Wernher Art Collection of works by Rembrandt and Titian among others.

If you are interested in animals and scenery the 43 bus will take you to the country extension of the London Zoo at Whipsnade, situated in the rolling countryside of the

Chilterns. White rhino, wild horses, hippos and lions graze in peace as the Whipsnade and Umfolozi Light Railway takes you through the large paddocks for closer inspection.

The train service to Luton is very good, there being a regular service with the efficient new 'Bed-Pan' units. For Tourist Information: (0582) 32629

As we travel north out of Luton the town's cosmopolitan nature is revealed in the distinctive tower of a mosque punctuating the skyline to the west with the Luton Football Club floodlights completing the vista.

If travelling on a H.S.T. the stations of Leagrave, Harlington and Flitwick pass in a flash but travelling on the more sedate electric units offers a better chance of admiring the scenery.

In addition to the TV screens that were installed for the driver only operation on the electric multiple units, all the stations have been tastefully renovated – the cleaned brickwork being especially pleasing to the eye. Of the three stations Harlington is the most welcoming with its hand painted 'Welcome to Harlington' sign, its well tended garden and trees presented by the local Brownies and Women's Institute. Excellent!

After Flitwick the line descends into the valley of the Great Ouse and passes the large clay pits that supply the nearby brickworks at Stewartby, to the west of the line. Meanwhile, in the east, clearly visible in the broad valley, can be seen the Cardington Airship hangars. These hangars stand as a monument for the last airship age which ended tragically in October 1930 when the R101 departed from Cardington on a voyage to India and crashed on a hillside at Beauvais killing 48 people. Airship Industries, who are based at Cardington, have led the field in a resurgence of interest in airships in recent years, part of the new scene being the successful use of airships to advertise products in the sky, such as Goodyear Tyres.

As Bedford station approaches the sight of firemen lined up for drill at the Bedfordshire County Fire HQ on the west of the line reminds one that Bedford is an important County town (pop. 73,000). Like Luton, Bedford's population is a cosmopolitan one, with a high proportion of Italian extraction, the reason being that imported labour was needed for working in the Stewartby brickworks in the 1950s.

Bedford (early closing: Thursday) is an ideal blend of old and new with the well renovated Harpur School buildings housing a new shopping centre. Further details on Bedford will be found in the Bedford to Bletchley section of this book. There is an excellent rail service to London and to the North – mainly H.S.T.s north and electric units and H.S.T.s to London.

If you are travelling on an H.S.T. which does not stop at Bedford, then no sooner are the southern crossovers for the station reached than the train is leaning into the curve avoiding the station and accelerating fast towards open country.

Once out of the environs of Bedford the passage north continues across the flood plain of the Great Ouse with numerous viaducts spanning the Oakley fox hunting countryside. The complex of buildings on the horizon to the east of the line at this point is part of the Royal Aircraft Establishment, Bedford, who specialise in testing planes outside and in wind tunnels, along with research into associated aviation projects such as conducting the trials for the Harrier ski jump platform on ships.

Seven miles out of Bedford, the now closed Sharnbrook station buildings appear on the west as well as the substantial village of Sharnbrook with its own health farm.

FIVE SHIRES BY RAIL!

EAST MIDLANDS RANGER

**SEVEN DAYS RAIL TRAVEL IN THIS AREA BETWEEN
9th FEBRUARY and 2nd NOVEMBER 1986**

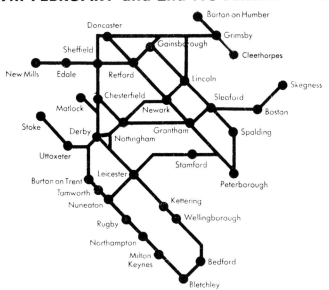

£19.00 Children 5 and under
16 years — £9.00

*On sale at most Booking Offices.
Not valid on the Rugby—Milton Keynes Direct Route*

We're getting there

Don't miss the train
tune into BBC LOCAL RADIO

258/476m
96.9/103.7 vhf
1161/630 kHz

1116 kHz 104.5/94.2 vhf

197/189m   1521/1584 kHz   95.4 vhf

271m   1107 kHz   104.2/103.6 vhf

There has been some local interest in reopening this station. The slow goods lines on the east gradually drop out of sight before they plunge into the 1 mile 100 yards long Sharnbrook tunnel. However, the fast lines go over the top of the hill on the steepest gradient of the Midland Line. At a rising gradient of 1 in 119/120 for four miles on both sides of the hill, it is not loved by faint-hearted engines!

The passage over Sharnbrook links the valleys of the Great Ouse and the Nene, and as soon as the summit is breasted it is downhill all the way into Northamptonshire and the town of Wellingborough. As the train enters Northamptonshire the town of Rushden (pop. 22,000) appears briefly to the east along with a working railway museum on the site of Irchester station. Very soon the rapidly descending train will cross the fourteen arch bridge in the valley of the river Nene and lean into the curve on the approach to Wellingborough station.

Wellingborough (pop. 40,000) stands at the junction of the river Ise from the north and the river Nene from the west.

Both Wellingborough and nearby Rushden dramatically increased their size at the end of the last century, mainly as a result of the establishment of the boot and shoe industry in each town. The Hind Hotel in Sheep Street, Wellingborough however, predates the shoe industry by many years for it was here that Cromwell is reputed to have stayed on his way to the battle of Naseby in 1645. Three centuries later, during the Second World War, its famous visitors included Sir Winston Churchill and General Charles de Gaulle. Ordinary visitors are still welcome at the Hind which provides accommodation, bar food and restaurant meals, along with Mann's bitter as its real ale.

For the visitor interested in shopping, in addition to the more conventional type of shops there is a new Arndale Shopping Centre situated not far from the Hind. Early closing day is Thursday. Unfortunately, at the present there is no bus link between the railway station and the town centre (¼ to ½ mile) so intending visitors may be advised to take a taxi. There is however a good bus service from the town centre to Earls Barton (4 miles away) where there is a 1,000 year old Saxon church tower which has been authoritatively described as the best example of its kind in the country.

Rail connections to Wellingborough are good with regular H.S.T. and loco hauled services throughout the day. Wellingborough station cannot be left without mention of its attractive Midland Railway (pre 1923) buildings and ironwork. Although the station is being renovated in its old style (modern working requirements permitting) the old signal box to the north of it, which has a great deal of character as signal boxes go, is to be pulled down soon under the Leicester resignalling scheme. Such is progress!

Five miles out of Wellingborough heading north there is a factory on the east of the line which produces the start of the day for millions – Weetabix! If you want to smell the baking in progress go to a vestibule, open a window (DO NOT lean out!) and hope the wind is blowing in the right direction. The Weetabix factory is situated in Burton Latimer which is four miles from Kettering.

Whichever way you pull into Kettering, whether it be from north or south, the restored ironwork and woodwork of the Midland Railway station deserve a glance of appreciation. The town of Kettering (pop. 46,000), like Wellingborough and Rushden, expanded rapidly in the last half of the 19th century as a result of the expansion of the shoe industry, and today it is the home of S.A.T.R.A. (Shoe and Allied Trades Research Association).

For the young (and young at heart) Kettering boasts a large pleasure park, Wicksteed Park, which is situated on a bus route in London Road to the south of the town centre. Slides, swings and roundabouts are free, and there are many other attractions such as a children's zoo, narrow gauge railway, and paddle steamer. Wicksteed ice cream is famous and in demand all year round.

Three miles north east of Kettering is the magnificent Boughton House, and just beyond it picturesque Geddington with the best preserved of the remaining three crosses erected in 1219 in memory of Queen Eleanor, wife of Edward I.

Returning to Kettering, the shopping facilities in the town are more traditional than Wellingborough's, through a small shopping centre, the Newborough Centre, has been built. Early closing is Thursday. Tourist Information Kettering 82143.

The rail service to Kettering is good with H.S.T.s and loco hauled trains north and south throughout the day. As the main line forges north away from Kettering the slow lines to the east peel away at Glendon South Junction and head towards Corby, whilst the main line heads towards Market Harborough.

No sooner has the junction and the village of Rushton, with its attractive closed station, been passed than an unusual sight appears on the west. Clearly visible from the train is the distinctive three-sided, three floored, three gabled and three everything Rushton Triangular Lodge. The lodge, which is open to the public, was built in 1597 by the famous Sir Thomas Tresham as a religious allegory symbolising the Holy Trinity.

After passing the lodge the H.S.T.s roar up the gradient through Desborough, which used to share a station with Rothwell – a possible case for an RDS re-opening campaign? – after which the train goes down the grade to Market Harborough and Leicestershire.

Boughton House, near Kettering. (*Photo* East Midlands Tourist Board.)

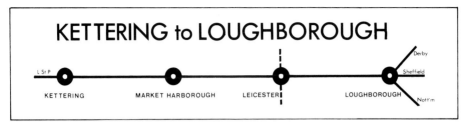

MIDLAND MAIN LINE
MARKET HARBOROUGH –
TRENT JUNCTION

by Darryl Taylor-Smith

Market Harborough, our first town in Leicestershire, is a beautiful town of 13,000 people. Founded in the thirteenth century by enterprising merchants, it is famous for its old grammar school and the fine wrought-iron Three Swans sign. It is central for exploring the upper valley of the River Welland, with beautiful villages like Church Langton, Slawston and Horninghold worth visiting. Another place of interest, to the northeast, is Hallaton, not only for its beauty but also for its annual Easter Monday Bottle Kicking.

Market Harborough station, tastefully refurbished a few years ago, was once a junction for Northampton, Rugby and Peterborough. It remains the railhead for a wide rural area served by a dozen trains a day each way between London, Leicester and points north.

The line climbs and veers northwestwards out of the Welland Valley, passing over the trackbed of the former Peterborough line, closed in 1965, and is soon running again through rolling hill country, reaching a summit at Kibworth. Trains no longer stop at Kibworth, which in common with other intermediate stations, lost its service in the 1960s. This is a great pity, not only for local residents, for the twin villages of Kibworth Harcourt and Kibworth Beauchamp are well worth walking around. Not far away is also picturesque Newton Harcourt, nestling alongside the mighty Grand Union Canal, which soon runs quite close to the railway, to the left.

Wigston Magna also had a station until 1966, and it should never have been closed, for the population of the combined Wigstons is well over 50,000 and still growing. The town is also known as Wigston Two Steeples, because it has two churches and was once two villages, one Angle and one Saxon. The line is now surrounded by houses as the great conurbation of Leicester stretches for nearly ten miles.

From May 1986, Wigston returns to the railway map with the opening of a new halt on the Nuneaton line, which now joins ours at a triangular junction. We then run down into Leicester where the station, in a brick-lined cutting, has been largely rebuilt with modern, functional platform buildings including a bookshop and two buffets. The entrance building, on the road bridge spanning the tracks, dates from Midland Railway days and is subject to a preservation order.

With a population of 284,000, Leicester is an important city with a lot of modern industry and shopping; but it also has a wealth of history and is well worth walking around with some lovely buildings and streets like Loseby Lanes, St. Martin's (have a look at the fine Swithland slate roofs, now extremely rare as the quarries are closed) and Town Hall Square. There is also an excellent market, open six days a week, and equally good and famous theatre, the Haymarket. For relics of the city's Roman origins, visit the Jewry Wall Museum; while the adjacent St. Nicholas' Church dates form Saxon times and the Castle Church from Norman times. There are further museums devoted to costumes, the Leicestershire Regiment, social history and technology.

As the train leaves Leicester, rail enthusiasts will note the busy locomotive stabling point on the right, and the new power signal box next to it. The view to the left soon opens up across the rooftops of the city towards the distant wooded hills on Charnwood Forest to the northwest.

The city's suburbs come to an end at Syston, a sprawling village, more a town now, which will hopefully have a station again in 1988, though served only by trains on the Melton line, with which there is a triangular junction.

Now we are in the Soar Valley. The train roars over Sileby and below Barrow-upon Soar – each of which once had a station. Sileby is a large shoe-making village; now large estates wrap around two sides like a crescent. The church is lovely, as is that of Barrow, which nestles alongside the Soar. To the east are upland wolds with attractive villages like Ratcliffe and Seagrave, while to the west is Rothley, with its Saxon Cross, ancient Bradgate Park, where the ill-fated Lady Jane Grey lived, and lovely Swithland reservoir – best seen from the Great Central Railway. It is hard to realise that it is man-made, with the swans, ducks and reed beds.

Between Sileby and Barrow-upon-Soar, on the left, is a Redland Stone depot, where Mountsorrel granite is loaded into hopper wagons and transported by train to many parts of the country.

Further on, also on the left, can be seen the Leicester Navigation – a canal originally built to carry coal – and soon after, on the right, is Loughborough Chord Junction, linking to the main line a remnant of the old Great Central route retained to serve the British Gypsum Works at Hotchley Hill.

Loughborough, population 45,000, is now more of the city than an industrial town. Famous for its Carillion and bell foundry, it also contains the Brush (Hawker-Siddley) factory, on the right of the line, where many British Rail locomotives and components have been made. Loughborough's former College of Advanced Technology is now an expanding university, noted for technological and physical education; while there is an equally famous College of Designs. Loughborough station was recently improved with the help of a County Council grant – the brickwork has been cleaned, the up side waiting room enlarged and 180 trees and shrubs planted on the station approach.

The train races northwards along the Soar Valley – prone to flooding in winter, but a new scheme should alleviate this – through closed stations at Hathern and Kegworth which used to serve villages some way off on the other side of the valley. Kegworth is the nearest the railway gets to the East Midlands Airport, four miles to the west at Castle Donington and served by buses from Nottingham and Long Eaton stations. After passing Radcliffe-on-Soar power station on the right, our train plunges into the short Redhill Tunnels, emerging from their northern portals (which have crenellated turrets whereas the southern ones are plain!) and is soon crossing the River Trent and leaving Leicestershire.

If your northbound High Speed Train has just afforded you this brief look at Leicestershire, I hope you will be tempted later to return to this beautiful rural county, famous for its Quorn, Belvoir and Fernie hunts; with historical sites and some of the finest museums outside London; for sports fans there are the Tigers, County Cricket and golf; and a wide range of theatres for entertainment.

London-Derby High Speed Train, seen here near Manton on a Sunday diversion. (*Photo* John C. Baker.)

MIDLAND MAIN LINE: TRENT JUNCTION – DERBY – SHEFFIELD

by Malcolm Goodall

Since the introduction of High Speed Trains (the Inter-City 125s), Sheffield expresses hurtle northwards along the Midland Main Line in record time. They burst through the short Redhill Tunnel and shoot confidently across the River Trent with its narrow flood plain, only to be faced with an odd problem at Trent South Junction.

Here the main line assumes a somewhat schizophrenic character. Ignoring the obvious route up the Erewash valley, most trains alternately fork left or right, as if unsure of the correct path. The reason for this indecision is soon apparent: east and west of the direct Erewash line lie the cities of Nottingham and Derby, each affording a traffic too important to be ignored by running due north. Nottingham is the larger city, and well served by fast trains from London; but few continue beyond it, because the Derby route is slightly shorter and better aligned. Thus the Sheffield traveller usually takes the western tracks, through the quaintly named Sheet Stores Junction. The line diverging southwards leads to Castle Donington power station, where white clouds of water vapour issue from the cooling towers. The brick warehouses on the north side were the central tarpaulin depot for the Midland Railway, but now their canal dock forms a marina for pleasure craft.

Some expresses call at Long Eaton, a busy suburban station with a large car park, and Barton bus connections to the East Midlands Airport at Castle Donington and the Erewash Valley towns of Sandiacre, Stapleford and Ilkeston. Shardlow canal museum is only three miles away by bicycle. Its ancient warehouses show the volume of goods transshipped between river and canal craft when Brindley's route was opened to the Potteries and Merseyside.

Beyond the M1 overbridge on the outskirts of Long Eaton are Church Wilne waterworks, purifying water extracted from the Derwent for distribution to Nottingham. The knowledgeable enthusiast may then spot traces of the long defunct Derby Canal near Borrowash, between the railway and the parallel main road which is of Roman origin. The rail-connected Courtauld's textile plant and power station are prominent to the south, with Spondon station conveniently adjoining. Industry then dominates the landscape and the route curves past the Railway Technical Centre where an interesting array of experimental and prototype rolling stock is kept.

Derby power signal box, just beyond, controls a large area including the main lines from Birmingham and Crewe which merge in at the southern end of the station. This key junction has frequent services radiating to London, Birmingham and the southwest; Crewe, Sheffield and the northeast, Matlock, Nottingham and Lincolnshire. It is very handy for workers at the British Rail Engineering workshops alongside and for the Royal Infirmary close by. Major improvements to the station buildings have recently been completed. The city of Derby is described on page 56.

Crooked spire, Chesterfield.
(*Photo* Malcolm Goodall.)

The 10½ miles north of Derby, up the valley of the River Derwent which the railway crosses several times, is described in the Derby–Matlock article on page 38. The junction at Ambergate was originally a triangular one and the station had three sets of platforms. Now it only has platforms for the Matlock trains, which diverge to the left, while the main line leaves the Derwent valley, burrows through two short tunnels and heads north up the valley of the River Amber.

The remains of Wingfield Manor then command the skyline over the valley on the west. South Wingfield village on the hilltop overlooks the church by the closed station. The classically designed booking hall still survives, though now blackened and neglected; its designer, Francis Thompson, spared no expense in producing this and other small gems of architecture.

The escarpment on the east side is the outcrop of the coal measures; one small drift mine driven straight into the scarp is still active, but other collieries around here are worked out and the mineral is mined at deeper levels further east. The Roman road, Ryknild Street, ran along the ridge between Derby and Chesterfield, surveyed in straight lines from one hilltop to another regardless of gradients; but the railway hugs the valley bottom until it has to resort to tunnelling through the watershed under the small town of Clay Cross. One of the earliest electric telegraphs on a railway was installed here as long ago as 1841 to give communication between both ends of the tunnel. Rich coal seams discovered during tunnelling led to the formation of the Clay Cross Company for mining and iron smelting.

The later Erewash Valley line from Nottingham joins ours from the east at Clay Cross South Junction, guarded by the prominent tower of North Wingfield Church. The importance of the coal industry is dramatically illustrated at night by the fiery glow from the coke ovens incongrously named 'Avenue' after the tree-lined coach road from Wingerworth. Smokeless fuel moves by rail from here to the furnaces of Sheffield and to domestic consumers further afield. A mile further on are long brick terraces of railway cottages in 'Midland Gothic' style, now sadly disfigured by their new owners.

Houses and factories herald the approach to the coal and iron town of Chesterfield. As a line from a tube works trails in from the west, the famous crooked spire of All Saints Church is clearly beheld. Legend has it that the devil flew down in a rage at the completion of another symbol of Christianity and twisted his tail round the offending spire, the deformity produced lasting to the present day. A more prosaic explanation put forward by cynics is the warping of unseasoned timber. By the small modern station is Markham's engineering works, which built many stationary steam engines used at local mines for winding coal.

Chesterfield, generally thought of as an industrial town, contains much of interest and is well worth a visit. On leaving the station entrance, just head straight for the crooked spire. Walk up Corporation Street past the restored Chesterfield Hotel, over the footbridge across the bypass road, calling in perhaps at the Pomegranate Theatre booking office, then into the church grounds. The church dates from 1234 and the nearby market is even older. A pedestrianised shopping centre leads from the church through thoughtfully restored streets to the narrow alleyways of the Shambles and the huge stone surfaced Market Place, alive with the bustle of trading on Mondays, Fridays and Saturdays, while a collector's flea-market is held on Thursdays.

Walk through the busy Market Hall and contrast this with the modern 'Pavements' complex opposite, a refreshing change from the usual concrete boxes. The 'Peacock' is a 16th century timber framed building on the Pavement frontage to the New Square end of the Market Place, beautifully converted to an Information Office open Monday to Saturday (Tel: 207777). A Heritage Centre on the upper floor is now open in the afternoon. A short distance further on, a footbridge leads from New Beetwell Street over the River Hipper to Queen's Park, whose attractions include county cricket, boating, bowls, swimming and tennis.

Chesterfield is a useful base for exploring the Peak District, using buses from the East Midland bus station in New Beetwell Street (Tel: 75432). All Sheffield – London trains call at Chesterfield, as do many North East to South West expresses and other useful cross-country trains.

To the north of Chesterfield is the hilltop Tapton House, leased by George Stephenson, the engineer of this line, who amused himself here in his retirement growing hothouse fruits. His North Midland Railway from Derby followed the valley of the little River Rother northwards to maintain its superb alignment, but our route diverges northwestwards towards Sheffield. A stagnant green ditch at Tapton Junction is the uppermost reach of the Chesterfield Canal, engineered by the pioneer Brindley to give an outlet for Peak District lead. After Sheepbridge ironworks comes a rural interlude with rugged stone-built farmsteads clinging to the hillsides.

Dronfield is a rapidly expanding commuter township with the old village as its centre. Its closed station was reopened as an emergency measure in the bad winter weather on 1979 – a move which prompted its permanent reopening, with an appropriate reorganisation of local bus services, in January 1981, with aid from Derbyshire County Council. Local trains call here but expresses hurry past on the climb to Bradway Tunnel, bored over 2000 yards through the millstone grit to gain access to the Sheaf Valley and a direct approach to the steel city of Sheffield. As the train slows for the journey's end, the well-kept Victorian stone station contrasts starkly with the massive 20th century Park Hill flats complex on the slopes above.

The city of Sheffield, with 547,000 inhabitants, until recently the centre of the cutlery trade and the steel industry, owes its origins to the existence of coal, ganister, fireclay and millstone grit as well as fast-flowing streams all in close proximity. The cutlery trade was established in the 16th century while about 1740 Huntsman produced the first crucible steel using local fireclay for making the pots in which the steel was smelted. In the same period, Thomas Boulsouver discovered the process of silverplating copper to produce Old Sheffield Plate.

The topography of the district meant that Sheffield was first served by a branch line from the North Midland Railway at Rotherham; but later construction has turned it into today's important junction, with services to the North East, South West, Lancashire and Humberside, as well as the Main Line over which we have travelled from London for over 160 miles through the East Midland Shires.

MIDLAND MAIN LINE: NOTTINGHAM – SHEFFIELD

by Malcolm Goodall

Nottingham and Sheffield, with populations of 300,000 and 547,000 respectively, are the two largest cities in this part of the country. For reasons mentioned before, most London–Sheffield expresses run via Derby and therefore miss Nottingham, but a frequent service operates from St. Pancras to that city.

The northbound traveller, however, heading for Yorkshire after a pause in Nottingham, will be somewhat bemused when his train unexpectedly turns south-westwards back towards London, until it suddenly veers sharp right at Attenborough Junction to head due north as expected. This is not due to the idiosyncrasies of railway geography but is a cost-cutting measure to prune Inter-City Sector mileage, with an accompanying time penalty. The internal saving to BR results from not having to use the slightly shorter Radford Junction–Trowell Junction route for Inter-City trains.

On a brighter note, the frequency has been improved to give a two-hourly interval service of new 'Sprinter' diesel multiple units calling at all stations, with additional trains between East Anglia and Lancashire and businessmen's High Speed Trains that call at Alfreton & Mansfield Parkway.

Nottingham's fine Edwardian station has been thoroughly modernised to give a good start to our journey. The train crawls out over the reverse curves that mark the site of the original 1839 terminal, and rapidly accelerates past Castle Park, a 'pop-art' piece of architecture for mundane warehousing purposes. Viewed from the air, its coloured gravel paths appear as a pinnacled tower! Prominently on the clifftop stands Nottingham Castle – a ducal mansion built in the 1670s on the site of the old castle which was demolished after the Civil War. It was burnt out in the Reform Bill riots of 1831 and subsequently restored by noted local architect T. C. Hine in 1878 as a museum.

Gabled and turretted Victorian lace magnates' houses can be discerned in the Park Estate to the west of the castle; while the Central Television studios soon come into view to the south of the line. A new station has been suggested here, to serve housing, industry, the Queen's Medical Centre and the University. Jesse Boot, founder of the pharmaceutical firm, donated Highfields Park for further education: the concrete tower block and older stone university buildings can be seen at a distance to the north. An international selection of containers at the Freightliner depot demonstrates the railway's important role in good transport. Boots' complex on the south side includes the original 1932 factory by Sir Owen Williams, greatly admired at the time for its novel construction, generous glazing and spacious layout.

Beeston station lies some distance from the town centre, but stopping trains find good patronage from surrounding housing and the Plessey electronics factory which manufactures telecommunications equipment. The nearby Shipstone's maltings are typical of many built to process Nottinghamshire sandland barley in the first stage of its conversion into the amber fluids which are well appreciated by players on the rugby pitch adjoining.

This part of the Trent Valley has extensive gravel pits with barges transporting aggregates around the flooded workings. Abandoned areas form a nature reserve with lakeside walks, conveniently reached from Attenborough station. Giant cooling towers at Ratcliff-on-Soar power station belch forth vapour in the distance to form a fluffy white backcloth to the watery scene, reducing the wooded slopes of Redhill into insignificance.

Our train veers sharp right just before Trent Junctions, through the lace manufacturing town of Long Eaton and past Toton marshalling yards, following the River Erewash. From Stapleford, with its curiously-carved Saxon cross, the Erewash Canal with its gaily painted pleasure craft keeps close company for several miles, skirting Stanton Ironworks which produces manhole covers and countless miles of pipes for water mains.

At Trowell Junction the direct line from Nottingham trails in from the east. Passengers on the occasional trains that still use this route can see the marina created on flat ground within sight of Nottingham Castle, then pass the Raleigh and Players factories that contribute so much to the city's prosperity. Where suburbia is left behind for open countryside beyond Wollaton, coal deposits were reputedly worked in Roman times. Profits from later pits helped finance the building of the impressive Wollaton Hall, completed in 1588 for Sir Francis Willoughby. By 1604, Huntingdon Beaumont had a wooden wagonway operating to carry coal from deeper mines nearby at Strelley – the first ever recorded railway in this country! It seems unfair that this enterprising pioneer's business failed to flourish; Beaumont ended up in Nottingham jail a few years later!

The small River Erewash forms the country boundary and is crossed several times by the railway, which means that potential sites for an Ilkeston station are in Nottinghamshire, although this important town of 33,000 people stands on a Derbyshire hilltop, to the west of the track. A competing route once strode across the valley on the spindly-legged ironwork Bennerley Viaduct, now preserved as an

Sun Inn, Eastwood (1 mile from Langley Mill station). (*Photo* Malcolm Goodall.)

industrial monument but strangely bereft of its approach embankments. Shipley Gate station has long since disappeared, but the older 'Boat' inn still serves refreshment to canal travellers in a rather isolated location.

The 'Sprinter' trains now slow to call at Langley Mill station, rebuilt and reopened in May 1986 with local authority finance. Walk from here down to the marina at Langley Bridge, formerly an important canal and now the head of navigation on the Erewash Canal. Continue up the hill for half a mile to Eastwood, noting the 'Sun' inn at the crossroads, popularly regarded as the birthplace of the Midland Railway. The controversial writer D. H. Lawrence was born in Eastwood and his former home at 8a Victoria Street is now a museum to his memory. Many of his novels are set in the surrounding countryside and mining townships. Walk the mile back downhill to the station or catch the frequent Trent bus which is the successor to the tramway which Lawrence used as the setting for his short story 'Tickets Please', later made into a television film.

Cyclists could take the Nottingham Road from Eastwood, past the 'Man in Space' at Hilltop, then bear left to Moorgreen and the hamlet of Greasley with its moated castle enclosure beside the church. Undulating roads give way to an easier gradient from Watnall Corner, over the M1 and past the 'Flying Bedstead' which commemorates an experimental vertical take-off aircraft tested at Watnall airfield. Another mile brings the rider to the mining and market town of Hucknall, where the poet Byron is interred in the parish church. If time permits, continue through picturesque Linby and Papplewick and on to the poet's home at Newstead Abbey, where his father, Captain 'Mad Jack' Byron staged mock naval battles on the lakes and even, it is said, fired a cannon at his unfortunate servants in their boat!

The train journey northwards from Langley Mill passes the restored grid-iron terraces of industrial workers' cottages at Codnor Park and Ironville. Trains of preserved rolling stock may be seen reversing here on the Midland Railway Trust's line, but there is no passenger interchange. Some freight traffic does however use a connection to reach the Butterley Company's engineering works. This concern used to have coalmines, ironworks, housing and its own private road and rail network; a fascinating hunting ground for the industrial archaeologist. Their best known product must be the framework of St. Pancras station trainshed, each girder bearing the company's name and date of manufacture.

Very soon, at Pye Bridge Junction, a heavily-used freight line climbs steeply away northeastwards, curving sharply as it follows the alignment of a former horse-drawn tramway. Railfreight locomotives haul successive strings of empty coal hoppers up here all day, for refilling at the collieries in Sherwood Forest. Many people wish to see passenger services restored over this line to Ashfield and Mansfield which, with a population approaching a quarter of a million, form the largest conurbation in the country without a train service. Until that happens, it is necessary for Mansfield-bound passengers to continue along the Sheffield line, through the tunnel to Alfreton & Mansfield Parkway station, built in 1973 on the site of an earlier, closed station with local authority help, and catch a bus for the eight miles to Mansfield.

Parkway station is also the railhead for the Midland Railway Trust's line and museum at Butterley; buses depart every half hour (hourly in the evenings and on Sundays). From here, our train has but a short climb to a summit in the mile-long cutting at Morton, and a quick descent to Clay Cross ironworks and junction, where the line from Derby merges in from the south west, overlooked by the blackened tower of North Wingfield church.

The remainder of the journey to Sheffield is described in the Trent–Derby–Sheffield section of this book (page 14).

Millbrook station, perhaps the most attractive on the Bedford–Bletchley line. (*Photo* Richard Crane.)

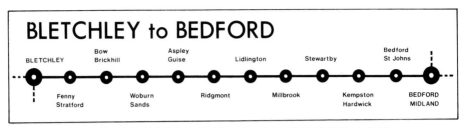

BEDFORD TO BLETCHLEY

by Matthew Gamble

We commence our journey at Bedford Midland, a modern station with good facilities. The diesel railcars used on the branch to Bletchley may look faintly quaint alongside the Inter City 125s and Bed-Pan electrics with which they share the station. However, they do carry prams and bicycles, which is more than can be said at the moment for the electrics!

Bedford itself is a thriving county town with a population of over 70,000 made up of an estimated seventy-two nationalities.

It is probably best known for its association with John Bunyan, non-conformist and author of the book *Pilgrim's Progress.* Bunyan was born in the nearby village of Elstow and spent most of his life in Bedford. Perhaps the town's main attraction is the Great Ouse, alongside which the beautiful Embankment gardens are laid out. There remains much pleasing architecture in the town. Bedford is well endowed with pubs, restaurants and hotels, and also plays host to a number of art galleries and museums. For tourist information, telephone Bedford 215226.

Back to the journey. As the railcar accelerates down the platform, on the left, we pass the site of the old Bedford Midland station, demolished to make way for electrification and to eliminate some tortuous curves south of the station. At the bottom of the platform our train leaves the Midland main line and trundles past sidings containing various items of rolling stock. We then make our way across the River Ouse, noticing on our left the fine Prebend Street bridge. Here, we are on the old Bedford to Hitchin line, closed to passengers in 1962 and used shortly afterwards for the making of the film 'Those Magnificent Men in Their Flying Machines' with an ex Highland Railway steam locomotive and BR coaches rather thinly disguised as a French railway train.

We soon veer to the left of the former Bedford to Hitchin line trackbed and enter St John's station. This halt was built in 1984 to replace the old St John's station when the line was extended to Bedford Midland. Although Midland is for the most part more convenient, a station in the St John's area was still required if the line was to retain much passenger traffic. Soon after the train has pulled away, on our left is the site of the old St John's Station. This was the first station to serve Bedford, being opened in 1846. The Bedford to Bletchley line was conceived by Bedford business men, who were concerned that their town, to be competitive, needed to be on the expanding railway network. By 1862 this line had become part of the cross country route linking Oxford and Cambridge. Traditionally the busiest section, by 1968 the Bedford to Bletchley line had reverted to its original position. Bedford St John's was once again the terminus on the branch from Bletchley, albeit now with less importance. Many had argued that services should be diverted to Midland and this was carried out in 1984, whereupon passenger traffic has increased by around half as much again.

Closer to us, also to our left, is a large pond, once a locomotive water supply but now a nature reserve. Having gained access to double track the train now accelerates through a landscape which changes in character from industrial to residential. In due course we pass under the Midland main line at Cow Bridge, and, after we have passed under another bridge, this time carrying the Kempston Relief Road, the chimneys of Kempston Hardwick brickworks loom into view across flat, open countryside. This works is now little used. The train stops at the halt, serving not only the works but also a small village of the same name.

Surrounded by arable land, the railcar pulls away. Ahead is the largest brickworks in Europe, Stewartby. After traversing Wootton crossing, we pass on our right Forder's sidings. Bricks are no longer despatched form here, the 'Fletliner' container trains ceasing to run early in 1985. However, Forder's sidings do handle two daily 'Easidispose' trains of containerised London rubbish which is dumped in nearby worked-out brick pits. With the abolition of the Greater London Council in 1986, the future of this valuable traffic is uncertain. Our train ratles on through the heart of the brickworks before calling at Stewartby halt, serving not only the brickworks but also a model village of nearly 1,000 inhabitants. Stewartby, begun in 1926, became a separate parish in 1937. It is named after Sir Halley Stewart, the first chairman of the 'London Brick Company and Forder's Limited', later shortened to London Brick Company.

As we trundle across the level crossing notice that the area seems more hilly now; emphasised by the excavations of the clay pits on our left. On our right, largely hidden from view, is Stewartby Lake Country Park; around three hundred and thirty acres of worked out clay pits set aside for recreation, of which two hundred are under water.

Our next port of call is Millbrook, one of the original stations on the line. At first there were five intermediate stations on the Bedford to Bletchley branch, viz., Millbrook, Lidlington, Ridgmont, Woburn Sands and Fenny Stratford. All except Lidlington were built in the attractive 'Cottage Orné' style – half timbered with all the features felt necessary for a proper rural atmosphere. Lidlington was built in brick and is not so ornate. We have the Duke of Bedford to thank for this, for although he was keen on the idea of the railway, he stipulated that the buildings should be in character with his estates.

Millbrook is now in private hands and is currently being restored after a long period of neglect. On the other side is a very substantial shelter of London and North Western Railway origin. The platforms are original (and rather low) so beware if alighting! This obstacle overcome, it is well worth alighting here, preferably with a bicycle. If you turn left at the level crossing, a mile or two away is the pretty little village of Millbrook. If you turn right, after a slightly shorter distance, you arrive at the bustling village of Marston Moretaine. This village boasts a sixteenth century manor house as well as a medieval church which has a richly carved roof and a detached bell tower – the latter is an uncommon feature in England.

After leaving Millbrook station, you may notice on your left signs which suggest that a motorway runs alongside the railway. It is no motorway however, but a Vauxhall test track. A little further on, we notice more sidings – these serve Lidlington tip where BR spoil is dumped in old clay pits.

The next station serves the sizeable residential village of Lidlington. Having left Lidlington, we begin climbing Brogborough Hill. The view at the summit gives the lie to the idea that all Bedfordshire is flat.

Once over the top we drop down into Ridgmont station. Ridgmont village, a mile or two away, is an attractive Bedford estate village whose church, like St Pancras station, was designed by Sir Gilbert Scott. After we have dived under the M1 and another road overbridge our DMU runs through pleasant countryside to Aspley Guise.

The halt is on the edge of the village, but it is only half a mile to the centre. On the way is the parish church which contains a medieval screen and fifteenth century brasses of a priest and a member of the De Gyse family, from whom Apsley Guise takes its name. It is said that Aspley House, built circa 1690, was constructed to the designs of Sir Christopher Wren.

One mile along the line is Woburn Sands, a busy little town. Some distance away are the town of Woburn and the neighbouring abbey, so visitors alighting at Woburn Sands should be prepared for quite a cycle ride. Woburn Abbey is the seat of the Duke of Bedford and is open all the year round. House and grounds offer a variety of things to see, from paintings by Canaletto to Père David deer, saved from extinction in their native China by a previous Duke. Woburn is a beautiful small town with buildings dating largely from the eighteenth century.

Having left Woburn Sands we approach, amidst dense foliage, Bow Brickhill halt, serving a pleasant village which is about half a mile from its railhead. A little further along the line we reduce speed to enter a single track section. The line was singled from Bletchley to this point when the A5(T) was built and a new rail overbridge was required to cross it. More colourful are the narrow boats on the Grand Union Canal which we traverse soon after crossing the A5.

We soon roll into Fenny Stratford station, serving a town long since swallowed up by Bletchley but which at one time, thanks to its presence on Watling Street, was by far the more important of the two. Bletchley only really grew with the railway. Fenny Stratford boasts a curious church which is divided into two parts, one half Victorian, the other much older but extensively restored in the eighteenth century.

After we leave Fenny Stratford station one rather rusty track diverges to the left; this leads to the concrete flyover, built in connection with a proposed marshalling yard at Swanbourne and clearly visible at Bletchley station. To our right is Bletchley motive power depot, at the time of writing home to the oldest locomotive on British Rail, a diesel shunting engine built in 1953 and recently repainted in green livery. We round the curve into Bletchley station where the branch trains terminate and connect with the Euston–Milton Keynes Central–Birmingham New Street semi-fast and stopping train services.

Since 1980 the Bedford to Bletchley service has been actively promoted by the Bedford to Bletchley Rail Users Association, formed on the initiative of the Railway Development Society. This voluntary group produces and delivers timetables and publicity of the rail service and have chartered several popular special trains originating from the branch line. Regular users of the service and anyone who is sympathetic to the aims of the association are welcome to the membership who are kept well informed of developments through a popular Newsletter produced 5 times each year. Full details are available from the Chairman, Richard Crane, 23 Hatfield Crescent, Bedford MK41 9RA.

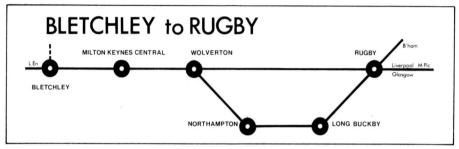

BLETCHLEY–
NORTHAMPTON–RUGBY
by Bob Mullins

As the D.M.U. swings over the pointwork at the east of Bletchley station the landscape change is profound. Gone is the rural scene and immediately ahead is the junction with the West Coast Main Line from Euston to Glasgow, Liverpool, Manchester and Birmingham – one of the busiest in the world.

Bletchley town is now part of the Milton Keynes conurbation (pop. 100,000) and although most of the town predates Milton Keynes it does have its new buildings, one of which is the Leisure Centre situated only a few minutes east from the station. Activities such as indoor bowls, yoga, bridge, swimming, netball and squash are amongst the many to be provided for at this modern establishment.

The existing towns of Bletchley, Wolverton and Stony Stratford were included in the Milton Keynes concept when it first began in the late 1960s. As Milton Keynes Central station is approached from the south the much maligned new housing estates and offices can be seen in full colour!

One of the most interesting places to visit is the new covered Central Milton Keynes Shopping Centre for which one must alight at one of BR's cleanest and most modern stations – Milton Keynes Central. This station and its surrounding buildings, such as the Stone and Webster House with its reflective glass, really give a spacious and futuristic feeling which is echoed everywhere in and around the new city centre.

To reach the centre simply walk across the station concourse to the main bus station and a 'Shoppalink' bus will whisk you into the centre. Well-known retail names such as Mothercare, Boots, Marks & Spencer and C & A compete with the West End up-market stores of Dickins and Jones and Lewis's amid surroundings of tropical plants, a pub and a wine bar (shops are open six days a week).

However, if solace is required then perhaps the Peace Pagoda in Willen Park on the east of the city would suffice, or a trip to the nearby countryside. The village of Beachampton, which is only five miles west of Central Milton Keynes and is on a bus route, is a quiet picturesque village off the Buckingham road with its own stream running through the main street and a really good traditional pub, *The Bell* (Greene King Abbot Ale).

Sitting outside with a pint in hand it does not seem possible that Milton Keynes is just across the fields! Indeed, as far as fields are concerned, look carefully to the east as your train approaches Wolverton station and see if you can spot the concrete cows! Wolverton however, to the north of the conurbation, is the part of Milton Keynes which has the largest connection with the railway, this being Wolverton Carriage Works which is to the west of the line.

The works is THE coach repair establishment on BR and, provided your train is going slowly, you may catch glimpses of different types and colours of coaches from all over the country. If you are very lucky you may even see the Royal train in its distinctive maroon livery, as it is normally stabled at Wolverton when not in use.

The rail service to Bletchley, Milton Keynes Central and Wolverton from London and Birmingham is hourly with, in addition, a number of Inter City services calling during the day at Milton Keynes Central.

The soaring spire of Hanslope to the east and the high speed junction of its name herald the county of spires, squires and stately homes – Northamptonshire. The West Coast Main Line avoids Northampton by leaving the slow lines at the end of the magnificent mile-long, 150-year old, brick-lined Roade cutting and heading towards Weedon.

Weedon became renowned in 1803 when the barracks, otherwise known as The Royal Military Depot, were set up by George III as a major control point in case of invasion by the French, the central England location being ideal for sending troops to any coast. If you are quick it is possible to catch a glimpse of the barracks to the west of the line, the graceful Georgian Cupola being especially prominent.

As the line approaches the old Roman settlement of Bannaventa, now known as Whilton Locks and Marina, two other forms of transport come close to the railway; namely road, in the shape of the M1 and A5, and water, in the shape of the Grand Union Canal. Rail, road and water all run within a few yards of each other as they pass through the break in the limestone ridge called the Watford Gap. On a train travelling along at the usual 90-100 mph it does not take long to overhaul the cars and coaches on the M1 as the two forms of transport run parallel.

Seconds later Kilsby tunnel envelops the train. It was a real brute to build. Started in 1834, difficulties were soon encountered in the form of quicksand which caused severe flooding. On top of this the contractor fell ill and only by the direct intervention of George and Robert Stephenson and the use of powerful pumping engines, 1,250 men and 200 horses was it finished on 21st June 1838.

Kilsby tunnel is 1 mile 666 yards long and has two enormous air shafts which can give the traveller the impression of going through three short tunnels as opposed to one long one. It can still prove troublesome, as after the February 1986 freeze-up when icicles weighing up to a ton fell on the main line from the ventilation shafts, causing extended diversions through Northampton.

As the line descends past the Hillmorton radio masts into the valley of the River Avon the line from Northampton reappears. They both enter the County of Warwickshire and the town of Tom Brown's Schooldays, the birthplace of Rugby football and an important railway junction – Rugby.

Rail services to Rugby are good with both local and Inter City services from London, Birmingham and the North calling regularly.

Northampton

From the south, no sooner has the crowded M1 been bridged than the dark of Hunsbury Hill tunnel shrouds the train. On top of the tunnel stands the tree moated remains called Danes Camp where some of Northamptonshire's first settlers – the Ancient Britons – had a magnificent view along the Nene Valley (pronounced 'Nenn' in Northampton) and it is here that a local ironstone railway society has set up a working steam muesum.

Modern-day Northampton is soon upon the traveller as the train descends towards the station. A quick glance to the west of the line reveals the 'Lighthouse' or 'Cobbler's Needle' as it has been christened – otherwise known as the Express Lift Company Lift Testing Tower, while to the east, the shape of the Carlsberg Brewery dominates the valley.

Cobbler's is an appropriate name because Northampton's fame once rested on its footware industry, which still survives with such famous names as Crockett & Jones and Church & Co. Back in the Civil War Cromwell relied upon Northampton to shoe his army, but in a generous display of magnanimity, Charles II donated 1,000 tons of timber towards the rebuilding of the Mother church of All Saints after the fire in 1675. Northampton station was rebuilt when the line was electrified in the 1960s and has all the facilities one would expect to serve a town of 151,000 population.

A short bus ride from the station forecourt takes one into the new bus station from which the ancient Crusaders' round Church of the Holy Sepulchre is a few yards north. Just to the south, however, old and new mingle on the cobbled Market Square (the site of one of the largest open markets in the country) where the ultra-modern Grosvenor Centre adjoins the tastefully reproduced 1595 Welsh House.

The venerable Angel Hotel in Bridge Street offers the traveller a nourishing platter in what was an old coaching inn, and by walking along Angel Street, past County Hall (part of which used to be the old gaol) the old and new once again confront one.

The little gem – the Victorian-built Royal Theatre (or the Rep as it is known locally) stands beside the brand new Derngate Centre which hosts anything from snooker to symphony concerts, and has guided tours, Monday to Friday (Telephone (0604) 266222).

As for spires, a quick bus ride along Kettering Road past one of Northampton's many open spaces – The Racecourse – and St. Matthew's 170 foot soaring spire comes into view. The church has cathedral like dimensions with the money for its building (it was consecrated in 1893) coming from a local brewer, Pickering Phipps. Inside the church is the famous Graham Sutherland tapestry 'The Crucifixion' and the Henry Moore sculpture 'The Madonna and Child'.

For squires and stately homes, nearby Althorp Park, the home of Earl Spencer (Princess Di's father) has a magnificent collection of pictures by Rubens and Van Dyke as well as an extensive collection of porcelain and furniture. Other stately homes nearby are Lamport Hall, Holdenby House and Castle Ashby.

The Grand Union Canal at Stoke Bruerne offers the interesting Waterways Museum and a good pub, *The Boat*, is located alongside the canal – handy for a contemplative pint of Ruddles while watching the amateur bargees 'locking down'.

The rail service to Northampton is generally hourly from Euston and Birmingham. Main Market Days: Wednesday, Friday and Saturday. Early Closing: Thursday – but many shops stay open. Tourist Information: Northampton 22677 (21 St. Giles Street).

Travelling north out of Northampton one passes the now closed Market Harborough line and goes close to Althorp House. In no time the small town of Long Buckby, famous for Golden Wonder Crisps and Maclaren baby buggies, is reached.

To the west, in the distance, can be seen Borough Hill with its BBC World Service masts, and then after two short tunnels, Rugby appears on the horizon.

Corbyrail excursion to Llandudno, 15th September 1985. (*Photo* Jim Wade.)

KETTERING – CORBY – MANTON

by Arthur Jordan

What must be one of, if not the, most scenic rail route in the Midlands is the line from Kettering to Melton Mowbray through Corby, Gretton, Harringworth, Manton and Oakham. Unfortunately this delightful journey through the Welland valley can only be made on the occasional Sunday when main line trains between Kettering and Leicester are diverted due to engineering works.

Leaving the main line at Glendon Junction one is soon reminded of the extensive iron ore quarrying which once fed the steel and tube making works at Corby, and so generated a lot of rail freight traffic, until the end of both quarrying and steel making in 1981. Passing the site of the steel works, now occupied by non-rail using firms, the branch leading to the still operative tube works, and along which steel strip from the North East is delivered by 'tube-liner' trains twice a day, can be seen curving away across an industrial wasteland.

Corby station, along with others along this line, closed to passengers in 1966 but the down platform remains from which, since 1984, three 'Corbyrail' special trains have picked up several hundred Corby folk as part of a campaign to get their station re-opened. After Corby the train dives into Corby tunnel (1,920 yards) and it was this and other excavations for the line by the Midland Railway in 1878-9 which revealed the extent of iron ore deposits, thus leading Samuel Lloyd to establish the Corby iron works and quarries.

Out of the blackness of the tunnel there immediately opens up a vista across the Welland Valley, once the grazing ground for hundreds of beef cattle before oil seed rape dyed the fields yellow. But it is still a magnificent view far into Rutland with seven church spires and a restored windmill along the skyline. The Northamptonshire village of Gretton, its station building now an electronic works, sits high on the Jurassic ridge which overlooks the valley and guarded by Rockingham Castle (featured in 'By the Sword Divided' TV serial). It was to Gretton station that Midland Railway dray horses came from distant stations to frolic in the fields during their fortnight's annual holiday.

Harringworth station is privately occupied and a delightful mini-Midland signal box stands at the approach to the viaduct, its block bells silent but ready for use in any emergency requiring single line working. The viaduct, variously named Harringworth or Welland or even Seaton, carries the line for three-quarters of a mile on 82 arches high above the valley and over the now closed LNWR lines from Rugby to Peterborough, Seaton to Luffenham and Seaton to Uppingham. Seaton's station buildings, footbridge and goods shed still survive, cared for, in a car breaker's yard!

Railwaymen called this line 'the rabbit warren' because their trains were frequently burrowing underground through the nine tunnels between Kettering and Nottingham and there are still five to Melton. At Manton Junction the Welland valley line joins that from Peterborough to Leicester, with the station buildings recognisable midst the sprawl of an engineering works, and the once prize-winning station gardens now covered by lupins and weeds. Beyond Manton tunnel one catches a glimpse of Rutland Water, a man-made lake, the largest in Europe, intended as a reservoir to meet an increasing demand for water which has not materialised! But the white sails of the yachts against the green of the extensive woodlands make a pleasant scene for the rail traveller.

Freight trains keep the Welland valley line's rails shining bright with the passage of tube-liners to Corby works, merry-go-round coal trains to southern power stations, stone trains for new road construction and tanker trains of oil and petrol. 'Corby Works' is the slogan of the local council seeking to attract new industry to a town with 20% unemployment. A complex of new roads connects the town to through routes and motorways but there has been no development of rail freight facilities. Not one firm has a rail siding, apart from British Steel. The volume of heavy lorries has increased to the detriment of the environment and the quality of life. What is needed is a determined effort to shift considerable quantities of goods from road to rail.

'Wonderworld', a theme park project promoted by a financial consortium, is expected to bring jobs and prosperity to Corby with an estimated two million visitors a year. For this British Rail is interested in restoring a passenger service, and extension of electrification from Bedford, through Kettering to Corby is included in BR's corporate plan. Whether Wonderworld materialises or not, a town the size of Corby (55,000) warrants a rail service, which is why local members of the RDS have formed Corbyrail to organise public support, and by running special trains, to demonstrate to BR the potential for increased traffic if they would re-open the station. Concern has been expressed concerning the difficulties business executives face in reaching Corby from the continent via Heathrow or Gatwick airports yet a fast rail service right into the town would be the answer, particularly when it will shortly be possible to run trains right through from the Midlands to Gatwick.

Harringworth Viaduct, at 1166 metres the longest masonry viaduct in Britain. (*Photo* Jim Wade.)

Narborough station. (*Photo The Journal*, Narborough).

NUNEATON TO LEICESTER

by Darryl Taylor-Smith

Nuneaton station is an important junction between the cross-country Birmingham–Norwich route and the West Coast Main Line from London Euston to the North West and Scotland. It is also a potentially useful junction for the important city of Coventry, if a regular passenger service is restored to the Nuneaton–Coventry line as the Railway Development Society has on various occasions suggested.

The approach from Nuneaton into Leicestershire hardly inspires visitors, with its views of scrapyards and the cars and juggernauts pounding the A5 road – here forming the boundary between Warwickshire and Leicestershire. Hinckley, the first town in the county, does not look too inviting either.

Yet first impressions can be wrong. Hinckley, while modern, does have a lot to offer: a good shopping centre, leisure centre and parish church. Markets are held on Monday and Saturday, while early closing is on Thursday. Hinckley is also a good starting point for exploration of some lovely countryside by bicycle. Five miles to the north is the historic site of the Battle of Bosworth where King Richard III met his death in 1485. The small town of Market Bosworth, nearby, is a real gem, as are the villages of Burbage and Stoke Golding; while at Cadeby is the only rectory in the country with a railway in the garden!

Between Shackerstone and Market Bosworth is a 2 ¾-mile steam railway operated by a preservation society on part of the old Nuneaton–Burton-on-Trent line. There is also a small museum with a fantastic collection of signals, lamps, poster timetables etc. For details contact: Market Bosworth Light Railway, Shackerstone Station, Market Bosworth, Leics. CV13 6NW. Trains run on Sundays and Bank Holidays from Easter till the end of September.

Some buses from Hinckley serve this area, but if you are travelling to Market Bosworth by bus it is generally advisable to use the hourly service from Leicester. On winter Sundays this runs less frequently, but on summer Sundays it also runs hourly and serves Market Bosworth station and Twycross Zoo direct.

Leaving Hinckley, the train passes through Burbage Common and gives pleasant views of a placid rural landscape. The next station, Narborough, was reopened in 1970 – the first Leicestershire station to be reopened by British Rail and, until 1986, the only one. Walkers and cyclists may like to explore nearby Littlethorpe, with a lovely old farmhouse; and Cosby, a conservation village with a tithe barn dated 1776 and a stream through the centre.

At Narborough you cross Leicestershire's main river, the Soar, and you can also see the embankment and viaduct which carried the former Great Central Railway southwards to Rugby and London. You are now in the outer suburbs of Leicester and the next station, South Wigston, is brand new, by courtesy of Leicestershire County Council and some active campaigners. At one time, Wigston had three stations, and indeed South Wigston was founded as a railway town and is very different from its older neighbour Wigston Magna. South Wigston was also the regimental headquarters of the former proud Leicestershire Regiment, the Tigers.

Within minutes of leaving South Wigston, we swing into the Midland Main Line and use one of its four tracks to run down through the suburbs to Leicester station.

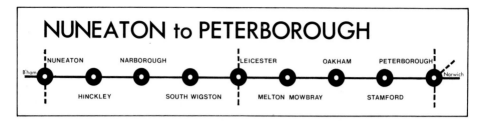

LEICESTER – PETERBOROUGH

by Darryl Taylor-Smith and Colin Hawthorn

This route is used by local diesel multiple unit trains and by four Inter-City trains each way between Birmingham and Norwich; as well as a daily train between Wolverhampton and Harwich and extras on summer Saturdays to Yarmouth. There are also four through trains from Cambridge to Birmingham and three from Leicester to Cambridge.

Trains head northwards out of Leicester on the Midland Main Line, from which the Peterborough line swings right at Syston and skirts the edge of the town. From here it runs up the fertile Wreake Valley. Man first made his mark in Leicestershire 4,000 years ago as he walked up the Wreake. Along its valley lie villages like Hoby, Thrussington, Rotherby and Frisby, all with lovely ironstone churches and houses and old brick cottages. John Fernley, the great nineteenth century horse painter, was born at Thrussington. To the south are the uplands with Burrough Hill, an ancient hill fort and racecourse, Pickwell and Gadesby. Between Hoby and Rotherby are the remains of the Wreake Canal, built in 1794.

You may explore these villages by bicycle from Leicester or Melton Mowbray. There are no longer any intermediate stations on this 15¼-mile section of route – although there is local interest in a reopened station at Syston (especially since the re-opening of South Wigston) and a possible new halt at East Goscote. Midland Fox buses on the hourly Leicester–Melton service call at some of these villages.

Asfordby, where iron ore used to be mined, also once had a station. This area will undergo some changes, of which the railway should take advantage, with the development of the Vale of Belvoir coalfield. Soon the remains of the Melton Mowbray–Nottingham line (closed in 1967 but still partially retained for research an testing purposes) trails in on the left. It was recently used for the staged crash of a goods train carrying a nuclear waste flask to demonstrate its safety.

Soon after the junction we run into Melton Mowbray station. Melton is a very gracious town of 17,000 population, clustered round the magnificent St. Mary's Church, which is well worth a visit. The town has one of the largest cattle markets in the U.K. They will sell almost anything, from a Stilton cheese to a cow, a ton of hay to a canary. The retail market continues to spread along the town centre and new shops are constantly being built. Pork pies are, of course, a famous local product, but the town is also notable as headquarters for the Royal Army Veterinary Corps, Pedigree Petfoods and a major shipping line (the sea is actually some ninety miles away).

Leaving Melton, Pedigree Petfoods factory is on the left, with a new siding opened with a Government grant in February 1986 to enable its products to be sent out by rail. The train soon rushes through the tiny hamlets of Wyfordby and Bretinby, past the site of watertroughs from which express steam locomotives could replenish themselves when travelling at speed. For this was once part of the main line from St. Pancras to Nottingham. There were also, in those days, up and down reception roads at intervals along the route, in which goods trains could stand while passenger trains sped past.

We pass the closed station of Saxby, formerly junction of a line to Little Bytham from where the Midland & Great Northern Joint Railway ran across Lincolnshire and Norfolk to Yarmouth, until its closure in 1959. This carried a daily Leicester–Yarmouth train and a service from Spalding to Nottingham.

We are also passing Stapleford Park, the scene of trouble between Lord Harborough and the Midland Railway, because he objected to the railway building over his land. For this reason the original line was sharply curved, and had to be re-aligned in 1892 when it became an express route from St. Pancras.

The line now bears southeastwards into the Vale of Catmose, crossing the border into beautiful Rutland, or Rotas Land, rich in medieval splendour, with buildings secular and religious. Farms, cottages, even barns are built of the rich golden local stone which skilled craftsmen fashioned into the glories of Oxford, Cambridge and the House of Commons.

Rutland was England's smallest county until its absorption into Leicestershire in 1974, when its County Council was reduced to District status. Oakham, Rutland's capital, with a population of 6,400, is a graceful, peaceful town with much to offer: museum, farm park with rare breeds, school, and a castle – really the Great Hall of the castle, perfectly preserved and used as the local court. Its walls are covered by horseshoes, but no normal ones – many of these are huge. By custom, every peer (and that includes Queen Victoria and Queen Elizabeth II) who enters the county must hand over a horseshoe. Oakham also has an ancient Grammar School, founded in 1584 by Archdeacon Johnson (who also founded the nearby Public School at Uppingham) and which has tripled in size in recent years. A well-known hostelry in Oakham is the Crown Hotel, an old building extensively modernised and with its accommodation increased.

Oakham station, well sited for the town centre, has two platforms, lengthened beyond the original ones and staggered towards the direction of travel. Even so, the platforms were not long enough to accommodate the 11/13 coach war-time expresses to Nottingham, Sheffield and, yes, Edinburgh, that used to call here, so that drawing up twice was necessary – which must have made it difficult for the 'Jubilee' engine in charge to keep time. The platforms will still not hold the present-day 11-coach Birmingham-Yarmouth summer Saturday through workings, but will just about manage the more usual 6-coach lengths of the Birmingham-Norwich trains. Most of these cross-country trains call at Melton Mowbray, Oakham and Stamford, though a few run non-stop from Leicester to Peterborough.

Should you be tempted to stay longer in Rutland, there is a long-distance footpath, the Viking Way, that leads over the hills into Lincolnshire; while four miles northeast of Oakham, at Cottesmore, is the Rutland Railway Museum, with industrial steam and diesel locomotives on an old quarry line, open to the public at weekends. To the

34

southeast of the town is Rutland Water, a reservoir with angling and boating facilities. As our train heads south through tiny Gunthorpe and down Egleton Bank, we catch a glimpse of Rutland Water to the left before plunging into Manton Tunnel.

At the southern exit to the tunnel is Manton Junction, the buildings of the now-closed station in the fork between our line and the route to Corby and Kettering which swings off to the right. A few miles away in the hills lies picturesque Uppingham. Almost every village in Rutland is a beautiful gem – especially Teigh, Tickencote, Market Overton and Lyddington with its Bede House, a former palace for the Bishops of Lincoln. They can be visited by bicycle from Oakham (but be prepared for hilly roads in parts).

Barton Transport buses call at John Street, Oakham and run to Melton, Stamford and (less frequently) Uppingham and Corby. For information contact their local office, Wilton Road, Melton Mowbray (Tel: 63291).

Our train is soon heading down the valley of the River Chater, and then the Welland, past lovely North and South Luffenham until, soon after Ketton Cement Works, we draw into Stamford, which sits on the boundaries of four former counties and, in character and history, would fit best into Rutland, although it is in fact in Lincolnshire. This fine old stonebuilt town, with its many preserved buildings, is described in *Lincolnshire by Rail*, as is the onward journey to Peterborough, a busy, expanding city on the edge of the Fens and a major railway junction.

The routes south and east of Peterborough are described in *East Anglia by Rail*, as is the Nene Valley steam railway – more than five miles of the former Peterborough–Northampton route, now operated by a preservation society and specialising in vintage locomotives and carriages from the Continent.

GREAT CENTRAL RAILWAY
by Reverend Geoffrey Evison

History and Background
The main line of the Great Central Railway ran from London Marylebone to Manchester London Road (now Piccadilly). It was completed in 1899 and was the last main line to be built into London. In 1923 the Great Central became part of the London & North Eastern Railway until 1948 when it was nationalised along with the rest of the British Railway network.

Unfortunately the Great Central main line suffered the effects of the Beeching axe and on September 5th 1966 was closed as a through route. Apart from the now preserved Loughborough Central to Rothley section, only two sections of the main line survive in use for passenger services. These are from Marylebone to Aylesbury and in the Sheffield area from Woodhouse Junction to Woodburn Junction. Hopefully, and funds permitting, the preserved Loughborough Central to Rothley section will be extended some 2½ miles southwards to a rebuilt station at Belgrave & Birstall on the northern outskirts of the city of Leicester in the near future.

When the section from Rugby Central to Nottingham Arkwright Street was closed on May 5th 1969 it provided an excellent and unique opportunity to preserve a stretch of main line railway. The preservation group formed under the name of Main Line Steam Trust originally intended to preserve the Leicester – Nottingham

Butler-Henderson at Rothley. (*Photo* Great Central Railway.)

section; but despite all the group's efforts and a public company, Great Central Railway (1976) p.l.c. being formed to raise the necessary cash by share issue, financial circumstances dictated that the scheme had to be curtailed to the present Loughborough to Rothley section. However, it is pleasing to note that circumstances seem to be changing rapidly and the original Leicester to Nottingham scheme, or at least from and to the outskirts of either city, now seems nearer to fruition than at any time since it was first mooted in 1969.

Three stations have been largely restored to their original condition, a museum has been established and steam locomotives from all four big pre-nationalisation railway companies can be seen, some working and some undergoing restoration.

Pride of place must go to locomotive number 506 *Butler Henderson* which is part of the National Collection and is kindly on loan from the National Railway Museum at York. The engine is over 60 years old and is the only example of an original Great Central passenger locomotive in preservation. More than a dozen other steam locomotives and some diesels are also preserved on the Great Central.

Every May the Railway holds a 'Schools Week', when hundreds of children from far and wide visit the line to be given a guided tour by volunteer guides and also have a journey on board the train. Except for a small nucleus of paid staff, the Great Central is run entirely by volunteers and new recruits are always more than welcome. For further information, write to: Great Central Railway (1976) p.l.c., PO Box 33, Great Central Station, Loughborough, Leics. LE11 1SS or telephone Loughborough (0509) 230726.

36

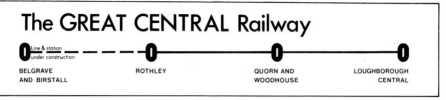

The GREAT CENTRAL Railway

| BELGRAVE AND BIRSTALL | ROTHLEY | QUORN AND WOODHOUSE | LOUGHBOROUGH CENTRAL |

The Line Today

Today's Great Central Railway runs through five miles of superb Leicestershire countryside. Loughborough Central station, the present northern terminus of the line, is situated approximately one mile from Loughborough Midland British Rail station. Central station has been largely restored to its original condition and a museum, containing many items of railway interest, is situated at the south end of platform 1; while at the north end of the station can be found the locomotive shed and restored working signal box.

The train journey to Rothley starts by passing under the Great Central Road Bridge and past the Ladybird Books factory on the left hand side. Houses can be seen on both sides of the line before you pass under the A6 road bridge and out into the beautiful Charnwood hunting country. Soon the village of Woodthorpe comes into view on the right before you pass under the road bridge leading to the village. Charnwood Forest can be seen in the distance on the right as the line continues on a rising gradient with rolling country on either side and soon you arrive at Quorn and Woodhouse station.

Here a loop is being installed on the right hand side of the station to allow two trains to pass each other. The station has been largely restored to its original condition except for the signal box which was bought by the writer and transported from Market Rasen in Lincolnshire. It is a fine example of a Great Central signal box and when restoration work is fully complete and the box becomes operational, it should blend in quite nicely with the surroundings.

After Quorn and Woodhouse, Buddon Wood can be seen on the left and in the distance the Mountsorrel granite quarries. Further views of Charnwood Forest, together with Beacon Hill, 248 metres above sea level, can be seen on the right as the train proceeds along the stretch of line known as the 'Quorn Straight', and incidentally still on a rising gradient. Then a mixture of both pature and arable farmland seems to form a patchwork on either side and soon the line swings to the left.

More wooded country can be seen before the line passes Kinchley Lane and very soon the beautiful Swithland Reservoir comes into view as the train approaches and passes over the first of two viaducts built to carry the line over it. Water can now be seen on both sides of the train as it crosses Brazil Island in the middle of the reservoir and then crosses the second viaduct. This reservoir houses the water supply for the city of Leicester and had to be drained to allow construction of the viaducts. A variety of bird life can be seen on it.

The line then crosses the Mountsorrel to Swithland road and passes the site of Swithland Sidings which once boasted a signal box and extensive exchange facilities. The overgrown remains of the trackbed of a privately owned branch to Mountsorrel quarries can be seen curving away in the near left hand corner and soon the line swings to the right and approaches Rothley station. This delightful station has also been restored and the typical GCR London Extension signal box presently being rebuilt on its west side came from Blind Lane, London. The station has a loop for the engine to run round its train before returning to Loughborough.

The extension to Belgrave & Birstall is now in progress, the appeal for this having been launched by His Royal Highness the Duke of Gloucester in June 1985. When this section is opened, the train will continue south across Rothley Brook, still on a rising gradient but more curved. Views of Thurcaston will be seen on the right before the line enters a deep cutting for about one mile to a newly-built station at Belgrave & Birstall.

At present, passenger services are operated from Loughborough to Rothley every weekend throughout the year on Wednesday afternoons from the end of May to the beginning of September. Excellent train catering services offer Sunday lunches and afternoon teas, while a luxury evening diner train operates on certain Saturday evenings during the year.

DERBY – SINFIN

by Simon Hartropp

This short branch was re-opened in 1976 as an ambitious scheme by the County Council to relieve traffic congestion by enabling the many commuters from north of Derby to reach the factories to the south. Typically there are just three trains on workdays. To join the select band of 'foreigners' who have travelled the line, you'll have to be up early!

Setting off to the south, our train takes the 'right hand fork'. Do look out of a right-hand window to admire the stone 'DERBY' implanted in an attractive flower bed by the modern power signal box. Ducking under the London Road Bridge, we enter the district of forge, foundry and factory. Almost any British transport vehicle has had some part made round here – look in passing for British Rail Engineering (Coaches), Williams Group, Ley's Castings (motor cars), Rolls-Royce (aircraft engines). Look to the right and behind after Ley's Castings and you'll see the floodlights of the famous Baseball Ground – home of Derby County (The Rams) Association Football Club. Almost immediately we stop at Peartree Station, convenient for Smith's non-ferrous foundry and the Rolls-Royce 'Main Works' and Materials Laboratories.

Once under the ring road, we leave the main line and curve tightly to the left to reach Sinfin North. Tucked in between Qualcast and NEI International Combustion, this station is, I think, unique in Britain as it does not have *any* public access – one can only walk to the adjacent factories.

The train continues down the branch to Sinfin Central. This site was a 'mock town' in World War II, set up to divert bombers from the Rolls-Royce, railway and other prime targets a mile or two away. As you can see, such diversions would be highly undesirable now! The mock town has been replaced by the very solid structures of the Rolls-Royce design offices, engine development and asembly buildings, and one of the most modern foundries in the world.

There is a public footpath from Sinfin Central, which will take you to the municipal golf course. The railway line now stops at the end of the sidings. This little branch was a regular over-night resting place for the Royal Train until the track to Chellaston was lifted about 10 years ago. One day, it may be a cycle and footpath into the undulating South Derbyshire countryside – but for now, the only way to Chellaston, Swankestone Bridge (where Bonnie Prince Charlie and Co decided they'd had enough of England!) and Melbourne is to walk the ½ mile to Allenton and catch a Trent bus.

Alternatively, the B.R. staff won't mind if you stay on the train and take a return journey through this heartland of British high technology.

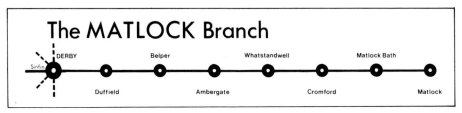

DERBY – MATLOCK

by Harry Pearson, Matlock-Sinfin Rail Users' Group

The advantages of a railway link between Derby and Matlock are so obvious that it may seem trite to restate them. We are so accustomed to travel by road that they are so often overlooked on short journeys. The smooth uninterrupted ride and the relative speed – 7 minutes to Duffield, only 13 minutes to Belper and 35 minutes to Matlock. And the frequency of the service is still such that it is satisfactory for many purposes (two hourly through most of the day with higher frequency at rush hours). One does not go as far as say Cromford or Matlock in order to rush back as soon as one has arrived. Moreover the cost is competitive with other forms of transport. Anyone can use the 'Derbyshire Day Discover' ticket, or if you are like me, retired, one can use a Senior Citizens card at half price.

In fact, however, the attractions of this valley route make excursions along it doubly enjoyable. If you drive, you cannot see much else than the road ahead, but the scenery from the railway is well worth looking at; also wherever you leave the car, there you have to return, whereas one of the delights of the valley is to walk along the route from one point to another without having to retrace steps.

Leaving Derby, the first stop to Duffield is soon over, nevertheless if going further there is ample time to enjoy the open view across the valley of the Derwent to Allestree and as far as the Water Tower at Quarndon which is a landmark for some miles around. And the view of Eaton and Duffield Bank on the other side makes you understand why this is a very pleasant place to live, and perhaps explains the extent of the platforms at Duffield station. I wonder how many people remember that there was once another railway up Duffield Bank, built by Sir Arthur Heywood for his own amusement to about one quarter scale with station, signalling bridges, tunnels etc. all complete. It was all sold and removed in 1915. What an attraction that would now be!

From Duffield a branch single line runs to Wirksworth which I remember using before the war. Unfortunately it now only carries minimal freight traffic. *The Wirksworth Phoenix* will rise again for the annual Well-Dressings however. During the spring bank holiday weekend there will be a special train service from Derby to Wirksworth. Don't miss a chance to travel by such a rare route to a colourful and historic event. More details from North Midlands RDS branch.

Incidentally the line here was built by George Stephenson for the North Midland Railway Co. in 1839 necessitating re-arrangement of the Turnpike Road between Duffield and Milford and the building of the Milford Tunnel to Belper. When it was opened on 11th May 1840 a great feast for all the workmen took place in a field in Duffield!

If you are quick you can see the Sighting Tower up on the Chevin that was erected to facilitate the building of the Milford Tunnel. But don't ask me how – I have read explanations but am little the wiser. Now we are out of the Tunnel again and crossing over the Derwent again. (How many times does the railway bridge the River Derwent between Derby and Matlock?) and running under so many bridges to Belper station. This is placed centrally in the present town though when it was built the general building was higher up, where it was supposedly healthier.

The railway through Belper is in a deep cutting, but it soon leaves this for the openness of the run to Ambergate, crossing the Derwent four times before it gets there. So far we have been running along the main line to Sheffield and the North but from here the line to Matlock branches off to the left. Some time ago this route was still the main Midland route to Manchester but sadly now it is single track and then only as far as Matlock. From Ambergate you will have the experience of travelling along a quite narrow valley with the Cromford Canal, the railway, the main A6 road and the River Derwent all parallel, all the way to Cromford. There must be few places left where this can still be seen.

The Canal, long since derelict, is a haven of wild life and a most enjoyable walk can be had by leaving the train and walking the 5 or 6 miles to Cromford along the Canal towpath or perhaps half the way to Whatstandwell. I personally always prefer to do it in the reverse direction – with my nose towards home so to speak.

Between Whatstandwell and Cromford the four routes mentioned above change their order in quite a confusing way. The railway crosses over the river four times, and the canal actually crosses the river by the Wigwell Aqueduct. Almost immediately after this you pass the Leawood Pump house which pumped water for the canal, and then the remains of High Peak Junction. This was the start of the High Peak Railway – wagons being hauled up the steep slope by cables to Middleton Top (where you can still see an engine house in pseudo-action) and then proceeding all the way as far as Whaley Bridge. There are benches and tables here which make it a convenient stop for refreshment on the canal walk.

There is a great deal of interest in Cromford, though the station is some distance from the village. The Arkwright Society has published excellent and cheap guides to both the village itself and the Canal, and has itself taken over the original Arkwright Cromford Mill, where many such guides can be purchased. If you look round Cromford apart from the Canal Wharf and the Mills, do not fail to visit North Street to see what wonderful houses Arkwright built for his workspeople. If you are interested in books, particularly second hand, then you should visit the Scarthin

Bookshop just up Scarthin Nick from the Market Place.

From Cromford you can also walk over the heights on the left hand of the road and river, or over High Tor on the right side, one of the above guides being for this purpose. The railway itself goes into a tunnel most of the way to Matlock Bath, but opens out in a comprehensive view of Matlock Town before entering Matlock station and the end of our journey.

One point – look at the architecture of Cromford and Matlock Bath stations. Matlock Bath was to be the Switzerland of England when the railway was built, and the station architecture reflects this.

WHAT TO SEE AND DO ALONG THE MATLOCK BRANCH

Few branch lines contains so much of interest in such a small catchment area, amid such attractive scenery as the 6¾ miles from Ambergate to Matlock.

WHATSTANDWELL

Nearest station to the National Tramway Museum at CRICH, a mile away up the hill. Leave the station by the footbridge, turn right at the road then left up a narrow road through Crich Carr. A collection of 40 tramcars from Britain and overseas is accommodated in a former quarry, with several available for visitors to ride along a 1-mile tramway with fine views. Open Easter – October at weekends and Monday – Thursday May-Oct. Details: National Tramway Museum, Crich, Matlock, DE4 5DP (Tel: 077-385-2565). Fairly frequent bus service from Matlock. Just round the corner from the Tramway Museum is Crich Stand. Erected as a war memorial to the Sherwood Foresters Regiment, it is usually open. The view from its top is breathtaking – but beware of the wind!

If you alight from a tram at Wakebridge you are well on the way to Florence Nightingale's birthplace at Holloway, and 3½ acres of Lea Rhododendron Gardens.

CROMFORD

Cromford Mill, the world's first successful water-powered cotton spinning mill built by Richard Arkwright in 1771, is open Wed., Thurs., Fri., Sun. all year plus summer Sats.

Cromford Wharf Steam Museum has a collection of stationery steam engines.

Cromford Canal – on summer Sat. and Sun. afternoons, horse-drawn barge trips are operated along the canal to Leawood Pumping Station, where the pumps are occasionally steamed during the summer.

High Peak Trail – a 17½-mile long walk and cycle-way from High Peak Junction, near Cromford, to Dowlow near Buxton, much of it on the trackbed of the Cromford & High Peak Railway, closed in 1967. Former railway workshops at High Peak Junction are open to the public at weekends, bank holidays and in school holidays. Three miles (and two inclines) along the Trail is Middleton Top with a magnificent viewpoint, bookstall, cine-corner, cycle ride and – at peak times – the restored steam engine.

Heights of Abraham Cable Cars. (*Photo* East Midlands Tourist Board.)

MATLOCK BATH

Heights of Abraham – cable car to Tree Tops Visitor Centre, Prospect Tower, Great Rutland Cavern – Nestus Mine, open daily Easter-October, plus restricted opening times in winter.

Derbyshire Toy Museum – open Easter-September, afternoons except Fridays. Also open winter Sunday afternoons.

Peak District Mining Museum – open daily all year.

Gulliver's Kingdom – open daily March-September – a theme park designed for families with younger children.

Aquarium – with many species of British and tropical fish – open daily Easter-September and winter weekends.

Illuminations at the Derwent Pleasure Grounds in the autumn to rival the more famous ones in Blackpool!

MATLOCK

Hall Leys Park, alongside the River Derwent with gardens, tennis, bowls, crazy golf, miniature railway. Indoor Swimming Pool. 15th century Parish Church.

Riber Castle – a ruin on the hill to the south of the town, with wildlife park, model railway, car museum and children's playground, open daily all year.

For further exploration of the Dales, or visits to Haddon Hall or Chatsworth House, Matlock Bus Station is 2 minutes from the railway station. Come out of the station approach, cross the river and bear left.

Matlock Railway Station contains a buffet and bookshop operated by Peakrail – the preservation society seeking to re-lay the line from here to Buxton – and a small exhibition.

Full information: West Derbyshire District Council, Tourist Information Office, The Pavilion, Matlock Bath, DE4 3NR (Tel: 55082).

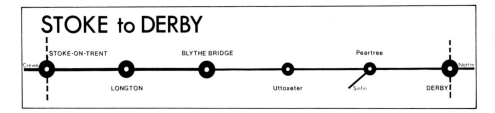

DERBY – STOKE-ON-TRENT

by Malcolm Goodall

This useful line provides part of a cross-country link from the coastal resorts and market towns of Lincolnshire, and the cities of Nottingham, Leicester and Derby, through to the Potteries and the renowned junction of Crewe, in Cheshire. After giving a spirited music-hall rendition of 'Oh, Mr. Porter, whatever shall I do?', the traveller may then catch a connection onward to Shrewsbury, Chester or North Wales; or northwards to Lancashire and Scotland.

The line is also popular with tourists and day trippers, for the Potteries are no longer the grimy Five Towns of Arnold Bennett's novels. The few remaining 'Bottle' kilns blacken the skies with smoke no more, the town trail footpaths lead along former rail routes and beside canals. Several well-known ceramics factories offer their wares for sale at factory shops and give guided tours to view their manufacture. Stoke City football ground, the Repertory Theatre and the Regional Film Theatre are all close to Stoke station.

The journey commences with a swift exit from the southern suburbs of Derby, out into the country and curving westwards away from the main line to Birmingham at Willington power station. The double-track line soon follows the flood plain of the River Dove, passing the ruins of 14th century Tutbury Castle. Mary, Queen of Scots, was held prisoner here in the 16th century. The church beside the castle has a fine Norman west front. Pastoral scenery continues, with occasional groves of poplar and willow unfortunately obscuring the view of Sudbury village and Hall which lie a mile to the north.

The approach to the small market town of Uttoxeter is unmistakeable, as the train curves round the racecourse to call at its now unstaffed station. The town has associations with Dr. Johnson (a sculpture was carved on the market place water conduit to commemorate him) but is nowadays noted for agricultural engineering. Uttoxeter is just inside Staffordshire but can be used as a railhead for part of West Derbyshire.

The route now twists and turns, passing through scattered rural settlements as it climbs out of the Dove valley. Blythe Bridge is the next halt, serving an expanding residential village and also giving access to the Foxfield Light Railway. The station of this former colliery line is half a mile away in Caverswall Road, whence on Summer Sundays and Bank Holiday Mondays steam trains with old-time rolling stock convey the enthusiast some 2½ miles to Dilhorne Park. A museum has also been established at the Caverswall Road site. Phone 0782 314532 for details.

The outer suburbs of the Potteries are soon reached, and just as soon disappear from view for a short interval as the train plunges downhill into the cacophonous black depths of the Meir tunnel. There follows an intricate patchwork of housing, industry and open fields characteristic of the area and a typical brick 'bottle' kiln appears on the right, as the train eases across a girder bridge to halt in the centre of Longton. There are no less than four ceramic factory shops within easy reach: John Beswick in Gold Street (Tel: 0782 313041); Melba-Wain, Heathcote Road (0782 319501); James Kent, King Street (0782 31931) and Royal Grafton China (0782 315667). A traditional early Victorian potbank in Uttoxeter Road has been carefully restored as a working museum of the trade, called the Gladstone Pottery, open seven days a week (0782 319232).

The Inter-City railhead of Stoke is only a few minutes' journey from Longton. Connecting electric services run north to Manchester, south to Stafford, Birmingham and London Euston. Confusingly, the city of Stoke-on-Trent, with a population of over a quarter of a million, is really a federation of Stoke itself, Hanley, Burslem, Tunstall, Longton, Fenton and Newcastle-under-Lyme.

Frequent buses run to the main shopping centre at Hanley, but there is plenty to see within five minutes' walk of Stoke station. Outside the entrance notice how the North Stafford Hotel was built in the style of a Jacobean manor round Winton Square to match the station and form a grandiose headquarters for the Potteries' own railway company, familiarly called the 'Knotty' from its coat of arms. Notice too the bronze statue of Josiah Wedgwood. Turn right under the railway bridge, walk over the bypass road and the 200-years older Trent & Mersey Canal, and there is a tourist information office in the Town Hall in Glebe Street, open Monday–Friday (Tel: 0782 48241). The Spode china factory, shop and museum are just round the corner in Church Street (Tel: 0782 46011). Josiah Spode perfected a blue transfer printing process on to earthenware in 1784, and went on to discover the formula for bone china, prized ever since for its delicacy, whiteness and transluscence. There's absolutely no excuse for drinking out of nasty plastic cups after a day out in the Potteries!

Nottingham Castle. (*Photo* Malcolm Goodall.)

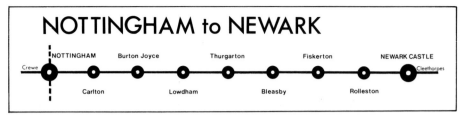

NOTTINGHAM to NEWARK

NOTTINGHAM – NEWARK – LINCOLN

by Basil Hewis

It was the extension of the Derby–Nottingham line northeastwards to Lincoln in 1846 which determined the present site of Nottingham station, opened on May 22nd 1848 to avoid the need for complicated reversing out of the original Carrington Street terminus.

The first train to run from Nottingham to Lincoln was a 16-coach special, full of dignitaries and champagne, taking just over one hour to cover the 33 miles non stop. Today's trains generally take just over an hour, but call at all, or nearly all, the eleven intermediate stations, and give an approximately hourly frequency between the two cities.

We leave Nottingham under London Road and over the canal, still used by pleasure craft but which formerly carried goods to and from wharves in the heart of the city. London trains also used to leave in this direction, via Old Dalby and Melton Mowbray! That line closed in 1967, and its iron girder bridge over the Trent now carries road traffic.

On the left, past the canal, is the old Great Northern Railway's London Road (Low Level) station, later becoming a parcels depot, but soon to be redeveloped for non-railway use. Thankfully, it is a protected listed building which has been majestically restored.

The once extensive sidings on both sides of the line are rapidly becoming redundant. Much railway archaeology remains, for about a mile, in the shape of extensive earthworks, derelict viaducts and bridges, which were part of the Great Northern's outlets from Nottingham Victoria and the two London Road stations (High Level and Low Level), and their connections with the Midland's empire.

On the right, the floodlights of Notts County and, just behind but across the Trent, Nottingham Forest (so hatedly called Notts Forest sometimes in the London press!) mark the two closest sited league football grounds in the country.

As we move out of the inner city area and over Colwick Road level crossing, we have a most interesting natural phenomenon on the left: a rare 220 million year old cliff face rock formation which has excited scientists and conservationists. Nottingham City Council has agreed to a request by the Nature Conservancy Council that the 40-foot high red-coloured face – made up of layers of rock and mud – is preserved. The cliff was formed in the Triassic period, when the River Trent was more than four times its present width, and Nottingham was an area of semi-desert.

On the right is Nottingham Racecourse, which also has an extensive country park. Just before the first station, Carlton – a busy suburb and shopping area – the

Grantham and Skegness line branches off to the right into Netherfield station. Until Nottingham Victoria closed in 1967, the Great Northern Grantham line ran separately but parallel to our line for two miles before taking to the earthworks previously mentioned. Then the above stations were called Carlton & Netherfield and Netherfield & Colwick – confused?!

The very edge of the built up area is marked by the bridge carrying the former Great Northern outer suburban line which now serves only Gedling Colliery.

The line to Newark is now straight and flat, passing through several almost equally spaced attractive villages – Burton Joyce, Lowdham, Thurgarton, Bleasby, Fiskerton. At Burton Joyce station we get our first – but certainly not last – view of the Trent, in a majestic 180 degree sweep. The low hills of the edge of the Trent Valley are visible to the right and left across the flat flood plain. The agriculture and the landscapes, however, are interesting and varied, with plenty of wildlife on view; mixed livestock and arable farms with small traditional fields and hedges; woods and extensive lineside ditches with marshes and bullrushes; old and operating gravel workings with extensive lakes; sewage farm lagoons. These stretches of water help to make the Trent Valley an important feeding and stopping place for migrating geese, ducks and waders, between the Arctic and European mainland.

The original station buildings at Lowdham and Thurgarton, in an ornate Tudor cottage style, plus the semaphore signalling, give an old world charm to this stretch of the line. Lowdham is blessed with a fine public house, inevitably 'The Railway', almost on the platform.

The appearance of 'Fiskerton Junction' on the signal box between Bleasby and Fiskerton stations may present a puzzle today, but this marks the spot where the line northwards to Southwell and Mansfield branched off. In fact this formed one third of a huge triangular junction, our line forms the second side, and the third was from Southwell southeastwards to Rolleston Junction – now just Rolleston.

Passenger trains first reached Southwell from Rolleston Junction (a distance of 2½ miles) in 1847, but a regular service was not introduced until 1860, thence on to Mansfield in 1871. Southwell station was then re-built and the original wooden building was transported to form part of Beeston station! The construction of the line to Mansfield helped to open up the coalfield in that area, and it was to cater for the coal traffic to Nottingham that the spur to Fiskerton Junction was opened in the 1920s.

The Southwell platforms at Rolleston are still there, untouched since the passenger service ceased on June 15th 1959. The area is now a riot of vegetation, young trees and colour in spring and summer, with wild and old garden flowers in profusion – in fact quite a nature reserve.

Rolleston is still the station for the adjacent Southwell Racecourse. The nearest station to the cathedral city of Southwell (with a population of just over 5,000 it is Britain's smallest) is actually Fiskerton. There is an unofficial service bus link between Fiskerton station and Southwell which the Lincoln–Newark–Nottingham Rail Users' Group is continually trying to tighten up.

Rolleston is the last station before Newark, and the last on the Midland Region before we move into Eastern territory under Doncaster management at Staythorpe crossing. On the right, Staythorpe Power Station, now partially closed, once received 20 coal trains a day, but switched to oil and then to road transport of coal

Newark Castle and the Trent. (*Photo* Malcolm Goodall.)

during and after the 1984/5 miners' strike. Needless to say, there is a strong desire locally to revert to rail haulage.

Just beyond the power station we have a spectacular crossing of the Trent near Staythorpe weir, where the river splits into two sections. The section over which we travel, the Trent proper, undredged, with several islands, sand and gravel banks, and of great wildlife value, skirts round Newark to the north; the two sections join up again a mile or so north of the town. The section which passes through Newark itself is partially canalised and dredged for river traffic – these days wholly pleasure craft. Up to the late 1970s, half a dozen barges a day, mainly carrying oil, were commonplace, and maybe in years to come some bulk freight will return to the water. But now, that oil is carried on our line, and you may well pass a rake of long tanker wagons. From Newark, trips lasting up to 2 hours can be taken in pleasure launches, with catering facilities, between about Easter and late September.

To the left of the line runs a long stretch of broad swampy ditch which is a marvellous wildlife haven untouched for decades. Then Newark is entered, past the livestock market on the right. Wednesday is market day, with cattle, pigs and sheep in great numbers. So important has Newark become for cattle that moves are afoot to seek a larger site. The castle is clearly visible behind the cattle market, dominating the river.

As Secretary of the line's rail users' group, the author is far from happy about the current state of Newark Castle Station. The main building is listed and protected, but has suffered from years of neglect and being boarded up. Until the early 1960s, the station boasted waiting rooms and a bustling café, and there is a determination locally, shared by British Rail, to bring it back to its former glory.

Castle station is closer to the historic centre of Newark than the town's other station, Northgate, on the East Coast Main Line. A short walk brings you across the river to the castle remains, dating from 1170, in attractive grounds which are open all year. The castle itself is currently being restored, although a small exhibition in the southwest tower is open on Wednesdays and Fridays.

Also worth a visit is the Millgate Museum of Folk Life and its craft workshops; while history and the present day come together in the large cobbled market square, with its stalls on Wednesday, Friday and Saturday against a background of many notable buildings, including the Governor's House, Moot Hall and beautiful 14th-century Old White Hart. There are bus services from Newark to Southwell and to Winthorpe with its extensive collection of historic aircraft.

As the train leaves Newark you can see evidence of considerable past freight activity – but the sidings are now lifted, and the coalyard and British Sugar Corporation factory now served by road.

Over the Trent again we go in spectacular fashion, over the weirs and locks on the canalised section, and on towards a very rare piece of railway engineeering – the famous or infamous flat crossing, which the East Coast Main Line approaches from the north on a latticed iron girder bridge. In the very early days, the Great Northern Railway was prepared to let the Midland control the crossing, giving the Midland priority, believing from the outset that the other company's traffic would be insignificant. However, friction persisted, and still does, over 60 years after the companies' demise. Drivers of today's Nottingham–Lincoln trains can still be heard to curse the !*!!* G. N. if they are held up by something on the East Cost Main Line, especially if it is a slow ballast train.

Beyond the flat crossing, we are joined by a spur from the main line, laid in 1965, which takes the Newark Northgate–Cleethorpes services and the daily High Speed Train between Cleethorpes and King's Cross. Shortly we go under the Great North Road and take a final look at the Trent as it heads north while we go northeast.

Collingham station, in an area of five level crossings within a mile or so, has an impressive building (now a private house) of 'Italianate-cum-Greek' style, in marked contrast to the Tudor style at Lowdham and Thurgarton. The desolate arm of a loading gauge and the earthworks of a loading ramp and bay remind us that goods traffic was once part of the life of this station. The delightful village of Collingham is the last one in Nottinghamshire, and the line passes into Lincolnshire, through gently undulating arable farmland, with stretches of woodland from time to time. Two more unstaffed stations, Swinderby and Hykeham are served, and we are then in the built-up area of Lincoln, with the first impressive view of that city's three-towered cathedral, dominating it to the north.

About two miles from Lincoln the train slows to negotiate a severe curve to the left, away from the original Midland line. This is the Boultham Curve, laid in 1984 and opened in May 1985 to enable the former Midland station of Lincoln St. Marks to be closed and all trains to use the larger and better-appointed Central station. The curve takes us on to the Doncaster line and we approach Lincoln from the west, over Brayford Pool, bustling with pleasure craft, and into the handsome stone-built Central Station. This was beautifully refurbished, with local authority financial help, in 1985, and is an ideal starting point for an exploration of the historic city of Lincoln; or for changing into trains to other parts of this large county.

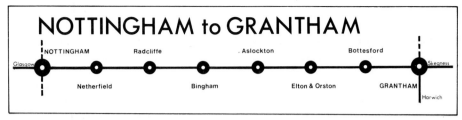

NOTTINGHAM – GRANTHAM

by Peter Wombwell and Robert Waite

The Nottingham–Grantham line is an important link used by a variety of trains – local paytrains and cross-country services, operated by modern 'Sprinters'; summer Saturday loco-hauled specials to the resort of Skegness; freight between the Midlands and Eastern England; and the daily 'European' between Glasgow and Harwich, connecting with the night boat to and from the Hook of Holland.

Some of the through cross-country workings are quite lengthy – from Crewe to Skegness, for example; while the current (1986/87) timetable has five through 'Sprinters' per day between Nottingham and the Lincolnshire resort.

The first 2¾ miles out of Nottingham are shared with the Newark line trains, as far as Netherfield Junction. Here the Grantham line, opened on July 15th 1850, heads southwest, through Netherfield Station, over Rectory Junction and across the River Trent by a viaduct, after which a freight-only line, opened in 1960, leaves ours and curves south to Cotgrave Colliery. We then head east to Radcliffe-on-Trent, where a 100-foot high red cliff stands next to the river and overlooks the surrounding countryside.

Leaving Radcliffe we continue to head east across the fairly flat farmland into the Vale of Belvoir (pronounced 'beevor'). To the north lies Newton Airfield. About halfway to Bingham was Saxondale Junction, where a line left ours and headed southeast to join the Newark–Bottesford–Market Harborough line near Harby. The Saxondale–Harby line closed to passengers on December 7th 1953 and to freight in 1962.

We then cross over the A46(T) by bridge. This road runs along part of the course of a Roman road called the Fosse Way between Lincoln and Exeter. About one mile north-east along the A46(T) is the site of a Roman settlement, Margidunum. This is said to have covered seven acres and was large enough for a garrison of 1,000 men. It is believed that it suffered much destruction by the Celts in AD61, after which it was rebuilt. By the end of the First Century it was no longer used as a military station, but continued as a town. Roman coins, pottery and other relics have been discovered on a site in this area.

Stone from the ramparts of Margidunum was used to construct the church tower at Bingham. The spire was added later and reaches 120 feet, dominating this little market town which has had several notable residents in its history.

The Rector here for many years was the father of Sir Christopher Wren, architect of St. Paul's Cathedral, London. The actress Lily Langtry often stayed at the Rectory. The author James Prior Kirk moved to Bingham in 1891 and died here in

1922. Today it is the home of Dennis McCarthy, the radio and television broadcaster.

Halfway between Bingham and Aslockton station we cross from British Rail's Midland Region into the Eastern Region. Aslockton is the birthplace of Thomas Cranmer, later Archbishop Cranmer (1489–1556), advisor to Henry VIII during his break with the Church of Rome. The Cranmers' Manor House, just north of the railway, has now gone. The present church was built in 1891 of Ancaster stone.

The railway crosses the River Smite half a mile east of Aslockton station, and we next call at Elton & Orston station which serves these two nearby villages. It was once hoped that Orston, half a mile north of the station, would develop into a spa resort, but this was not to be. The earliest part of its church dates form the 13th century. In a recess in the wall is placed a drum from the Battle of Waterloo.

Elton is three quarters of a mile south of the station. The church of St. Michael and All Angels here is only 15 feet wide. In 1780, the verger dug up 200 silver pennies dating from Henry II's reign, from the churchyard. There was a similar incident at Orston when 1,500 coins from the Civil War were unearthed in 1952.

Halfway between Elton & Orston and Bottesford stations, we cross from Nottinghamshire into the northernmost tip of Leicestershire and see the remains of the Newark–Market Harborough route, otherwise known as the Great Northern and London & North Western Joint Railway. The northern section of this is still open to freight trains, from Newark, and is connected to our line by a west-facing junction at Bottesford West Junction. South of here, the GN & LNW Joint was closed to passengers on December 7th 1953, although it remained in use for excursions from Leicester's former Belgrave Road station to Skegness and Mablethorpe until September 9th 1962.

Shortly after the junction we cross over the River Devon and then find ourselves in Bottesford, the most northerly village in Leicestershire with the largest village church in the county. It also has the county's tallest spire, reaching 210 feet. There are memorials to eight Earls of Rutland in the building.

On a clear day it is possible to see Belvoir Castle, situated on a hill overlooking the surrounding countryside, three miles south of the railway. The present castle is built on the site of a mediaeval fortress and has been extensively rebuilt during the 17th, 18th and 19th centuries. It has been the seat of the Dukes of Rutland since Henry VIII's time. The castle is open to the public and special events include mediaeval Jousting Tournaments.

Belvoir Castle can be reached by bus from the Red Lion public house in Bottesford. Barton Transport service no. 129 to Melton Mowbray calls there four to five times a day (not Sundays). For details contact Barton Transport, Wilton Road, Melton Mowbray, Leics. (Tel: 63291). Alternatively, you can cycle there from Bottesford or one of the other stations on the line, perhaps visiting en route some of the historic churches of the Vale of Belvoir.

The train heads eastwards, passing 1 ½ miles beyond Bottesford, Belvoir Junction where a freight-only line left ours and headed south to Denton. This was used by trains carrying ironstone until the branch closed in 1973.

Next comes the site of Sedgebrook station, closed to passengers on July 2nd 1956, and a mile further on Allington Junction, where the Grantham Avoiding Line, opened in 1875, curves away to our left. This is used by freight trains, typically carrying imported steel from Boston Docks to the Midlands, and by summer passenger trains to Skegness.

Our line heads southwest, under the Great North Road and through the quarter-mile Gonerby Tunnel. The town of Grantham is now ahead of us, and we curve round into its station, which has just undergone a £500,000 improvement scheme, involving new buildings on the down platform and extensive refurbishing on the up side.

At Grantham, a pleasant town surrounded by hills, you can admire St. Wulfram's church with its soaring spire, gaze at the birthplace of Margaret Thatcher on the corner of North Parade, shop in the busy market or the Isaac Newton centre, drink in old coaching inns. It's worth stopping off here before, perhaps, continuing your explorations by rail north or south on the East Coast Main Line, or eastwards into the heart of Lincolnshire.

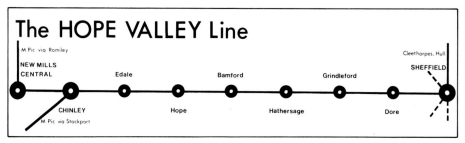

The HOPE VALLEY Line

HOPE VALLEY LINE

by Denis Bradbury

The Hope Valley Line was one of the last major lines in the country to be built, being completed in 1893, nearly fifty years after the more northerly Woodhead line between Sheffield and Manchester which had been opened in December 1845. This was due to the vast expense of the heavy engineering work involved in building the route.

In 1872, the Midland Railway promoted a line from Sheffield to Bakewell, but did not go ahead with it; however, finding that it was losing heavily to its competitors, the Midland decided in 1888 to build a direct line from Dore to Chinley, where it joined up with the Manchester to Derby line.

On leaving Sheffield Midland station, the train travels up the valley of the River Sheaf at a steady gradient of 1 in 100 for eight miles up to the summit in Totley Tunnel.

Four miles from Sheffield, the Hope Valley Line branches off from the main line to Chesterfield. At this point, the train passes the Abbeydale Industrial Hamlet on the right hand side. This unique 18th century works is the only surviving relic of the original cutlery industry of Sheffield, which was situated in the Sheaf Valley. The hamlet, which is open throughout the year except on Christmas Day, contains crucible melting furnaces, water-driven forges, grinding shops and blacksmith's shops, cottages and warehouses. The mill dam at the side of the line provides the water power for the wheels.

Not far away are the remains of Beauchief Abbey, founded in 1175; only the western tower remains, but it is still used for church services on Sundays.

Just before reaching Dore station, the train crosses the River Limb as it flows into the Sheaf. The river formerly marked the boundary between the Saxon kingdom of Northumbria and Wessex, and it was also a county and diocesan boundary.

Dore station, formerly Dore & Totley station, was once an important junction, but has been sadly butchered by British Rail and reduced to a single platform. The station was built following an agreement between the Duke of Devonshire, who owned most of the surrounding land, and the Midland Railway.

A mile away up the hill to the right of the line is the village of Dore. In the year 827, a treaty was signed here between Egbert, king of Mercia, and Eanred, king of Northumbria, which made Egbert king of the whole English-speaking race from the Firth of Forth to the English Channel, and thus brought about the union of England.

About a mile and a half beyond Dore station, the train enters Totley Tunnel. A board at the entrance states that the tunnel is 6230 yards long, the second longest tunnel in Britain. It took four years to build this tunnel, the navvies working on it having to contend with vast quantities of water. At one time during the construction, 26,000 gallons of water were being pumped out every hour. At the time of the construction it was said that every navvy working in the tunnel was like Moses – whenever he struck the rock, water gushed out. Water is still a considerable problem in the tunnel today, involving British Rail in a good deal of maintenance.

Apart from the water troubles, the major landowners under whose land the tunnel was driven had to be placated. The Duke of Rutland claimed that the tunnel would interfere whith his grouse shooting on the Moors above, and all work in the tunnel was suspended between August 12th and October 1st – the shooting season.

The train emerges from the tunnel at Grindleford in the Derwent Valley. Above this village, millstones were cut out of the living rock and sold all over the country to grind grain. Unfinished stones can still be found in various quarries. Grindleford is the first of several North Derbyshire stations on the line at which, particularly at weekends, you can see citydwellers alighting with rucksacks and walking boots to explore the moors and dales. On the right hand side near the station is Padley Chapel – a stone building used for many years as a cattle shed. The Chapel belonged to Padley Hall, the seat of the Eyre family who were staunch Catholics.

In 1588, during a search, two Catholic priests were found hiding in the Hall. They were taken to Derby and hanged, drawn and quartered for the crime of being priests and thus traitors to Queen Elizabeth the First. John Fitzherbert, who was living in the Hall at the time, was also put to death and the estates confiscated.

Some four miles southwest of Grindleford is the village of Eyam, which can be reached by bus. In 1655, the plague broke out in the village, thought to have come from London in a box of clothes. The villagers went into voluntary isolation and most of them died during the ensuing year. The full story of the Plague is set out in the Parish Church and neighbouring houses.

From Grindleford the line turns northwards alongside the River Derwent to Hathersage – a pleasant little town which is mentioned in Charlotte Bronte's *Jane Eyre* under the name of Morton. In Hathersage can be seen the grave of 'Little John', friend of Robin Hood. The grave is some ten feet long.

The next station along the line is Bamford, where the train crosses the River

Derwent as it flows from the Derwent Valley Water Board's reservoirs a few miles to the north. The reservoirs, which extend for some six miles up the valley, supply water to Sheffield, Derby, Nottingham and Leicester. Ladybower, the nearest reservoir, is about two miles from Bamford station and the dam can be seen briefly from the train. There is a sparse bus service in the summer between Bamford and the Ladybower reservoir.

Some two miles west of Bamford is Hope, which is also the station for Castleton, and a reasonably frequent bus service runs between the two.

The limestone hills surrounding Castleton contain four interesting sets of caves. These comprise the Peak Cavern and Treak Cavern; the Speedwell mine, which is visited by a trip in a boat along an underground canal built to drain water from the mine; and, higher up on the hillside the Blue John Mine where the famous Blue John rock is obtained. Above Castleton stands the ruin of Peveril Castle, dating from the time of William the Conqueror and woven into Scott's *Peveril of the Peak.*

From Hope station the line climbs on a steady gradient of 1 in 100 to the summit in Cowburn Tunnel, following the course of the River Noe. As the line leaves Hope, a freight branch runs off to the left on its way to Earl's Cement Works on the far side of the valley. The Works can be seen in the distance, the 300 foot chimney being one of the tallest in England.

At the head of the valley is Edale station, a favourite centre for tourists and hikers and the southern end of the Pennine Way, which stretches for some 250 miles along the summit of the Pennines to Kirk Yetholm on the northern slopes of the Cheviots.

Beyond Edale village is Kinder Scout, generally known as 'The Peak'. It is a featureless plateau of heather and peat, several square miles in area, 2088 feet above sea level at its highest point. No place to be caught in a mist without a compass and map! Here mention may be made of the 'Mass Trespass' by hundreds of people onto Kinder Scout on April 4th 1932 in support of the Access to Mountains Bill, which had been regularly rejected by Parliament since it was first introduced in 1888.

The demonstrators were met by a strong force of police and gamekeepers. Five ramblers were arrested and sentenced at Derby Assizes to between two and six months' imprisonment. The Bill finally became law some years later and opened the moorlands to the public for the greater part of the year.

The traveller may well wonder why a flat-topped hill should be called The Peak. The name of the Peak District given to this part of the Pennines has nothing to do with the shape of the hills, but derives from Pecsetan, the name of a Celtic tribe who lived in this area in pre-Roman times. Over the centuries, Pecsetan was changed into Peak.

Shortly after leaving Edale, the train enters Cowburn Tunnel, 3702 yards long and 875 feet below the moor. It has the distinction of being the deepest tunnel on any British railway. One night during the 1914-18 war, the driver and fireman of a train approaching Cowburn Tunnel realised that they were being shadowed by a German Zeppelin. Once the train had entered the tunnel it came to a halt and remained in the tunnel for a considerable time until the loco crew were satisfied that the Zeppelin, having lost the train, had gone away.

From the western portal of Cowburn Tunnel, the train travels a further three miles to Chinley, passing the triangular junction with the former Midland main line to Derby on the left. This line now goes to Buxton only and is heavily used by freight from the extensive ICI limestone quarries at Peak Dale.

Locomotive 47512 emerges from Cowburn Tunnel with an Inter-City train.
(*Photo* Tom Heaviside.)

In the summer of 1985 this route was used by weekend DMU services in connection with Peakrail's preservation scheme at Buxton. Normally, would-be rail travellers from Sheffield to the Derbyshire resort of Buxton must alight at New Mills Central and walk half a mile to New Mills Newtown station, which has an hourly service to Buxton.

As the Hope Valley train approaches Chinley Station, one can look back on the right hand side and see the Cowburn Tunnel ventilator, high up on the moorland skyline. Chinley station itself, 700 feet above sea level, must rank as one of the coldest in the country on which to wait for a train. It was once an important junction, but has suffered the same fate as Dore & Totley.

From Chinley, the line follows the valleys of the Black Brook and the River Goyt. Local trains then fork right, bridging two gorges and piercing an intervening rock at the approach to New Mills Central and Manchester via Romiley. Longer-distance trains to Stockport, Manchester and beyond have, since May 1986, taken the left-hand fork, which plunges into the gloom of yet another long tunnel (Disley, 3866 yards in length) and over a new chord line at Hazel Grove to Stockport (where Buxton line trains also call), Manchester and Liverpool. This modest investment by British Rail sensibly knits together unco-ordinated lines inherited from competing companies.

Whichever route one takes, Derbyshire has now been left behind and the train has reached what was formerly Cheshire and is now part of Greater Manchester. Routes and places of interest west of here are described in our companion volume, *Cheshire and North Wales by Rail*.

PEAK RAIL

by John Snell (Chairman, Peak Rail (Operations) Ltd.)

Peak Rail was formed in the mid 1970s with the aim of reconstructing and operating the closed section of the Midland Railway's Derby–Manchester route between Matlock and Buxton. The organisation comprises an enthusiast society, the Peak Railway Society with a membership of approximately 1500, and an operating company, Peak Rail (Operations) Ltd., which has some 400 shareholders.

Peak Rail Operations owns the 3 acre Buxton Midland Station site where a thriving steam centre has been established. The Company also leases land and buildings from BR and West Derbyshire District Council at Matlock station; where a shop, café and loco restoration building have been developed, and from West Derbyshire District Council at Darley Dale where the up side station building and platform are being renovated.

Since 1979 a number of attempts have been made to obtain planning permission for the whole 20-mile route, but on each occasion these have been rejected on the highway safety grounds, the Highway Authorities fearing that road access and parking provision would be inadequate for the scale of project envisaged. However, early in 1986, West Derbyshire District Council did give planning permission on a 5-year basis for the Matlock–Darley Dale section and it is hoped that the other authorities concerned will now follow suit. Obstacles still remain, as West Derbyshire have not yet agreed to a lease on the section of trackbed which they own, and other local interests are lobbying for it to be used as an industrial access road in Darley Dale. This topic was recently debated in front of a Department of the Environment Inspector at the Matlock Local Plan Public Enquiry.

In 1979–81, Peak Rail operated a charter public Sunday service on the Derby–Matlock line. This demonstrated the viability of the service and in 1982 it was taken over on a revenue support basis by Derbyshire County Council. From 1983 to date it has been wholly operated by BR, without any revenue support.

The section of the Matlock–Buxton line between Buxton and Blackwell Mill (3¾ miles) is still operated by BR as a freight line to service the extensive quarries between Blackwell Mill and Chinley. In 1985, Peak Rail operated a profit-sharing DMU service with BR over this line as part of a Buxton–New Mills Central public service (Sundays only), making connections with Hope Valley trains. The service, called 'The Peak Rail Rambler' was extremely successful and did not need to call on the revenue guarantee offered by Derbyshire County Council. The service will run again in 1986, this time as a Peak Rail charter, on every Sunday in July and August, the first two in September and August Bank Holiday Monday. The middle train of the three may possibly be routed via the Hazel Grove Chord.

Agreement has recently been reached with BR to construct a halt at Blackwell Mill for the 1987 season.

At Buxton, a grant of £30,000 has recently been received from Greater Manchester Council to assist in replacing the missing bridge which separates Buxton Midland station from the Ashwood Dale line. This project is scheduled for completion in the autumn and, following completion of a junction agreement with BR, the 'Rambler' service then will be able to operate from Midland station.

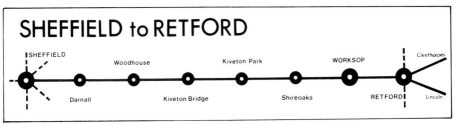

SHEFFIELD – RETFORD

by Devon Baillie

Passenger trains from Sheffield to Retford, Cleethorpes and Lincoln run for the first ten miles through industrial South Yorkshire, sharing the route with steady freight traffic. After Kiveton Park, the line crosses into Nottinghamshire's more rural Bassetlow District. To the right, the Chesterfield canal comes into view and becomes navigable east of Worksop. Just over the hill to the north is the Lindrick Golf course, scene of the British Ryder Cup victory over the USA in 1957 – a feat so rare it was not achieved again until a combined British and European team won in 1985.

Shireoaks is a pleasant stone-built village by the River Ryton, on which there is a ford, with a seventeenth century hall nearby. Just beyond Shireoaks station is a triangular junction with a line which is now freight-only, for 'Merry-go-Round' coal trains from a number of central Nottinghamshire collieries, but which was used by a passenger service from Nottingham to Worksop via Hucknall, Mansfield and Shirebrook, until it was killed off by Dr. Beeching. With goods sidings on either side, a Tesco superstore on the left, a wagon repair shed on the right, we draw into Worksop.

Worksop is the largest station on the line, serving a town of 37,000population and the only one still fully staffed. Worksop station's architecture reassembles that of a Jacobean manor house and is a fitting gateway to the town, which contains some imposing Georgian and Victorian buildings and the fine Priory Church and Gatehouse dating from Norman times. Worksop also has a thriving market, and can be a useful starting point for cycling trips southwards to Welbeck Abbey, Sherwood Forest and Clumber Park – the last of these being 4000 acres of parkland, woodland and a lake, open to the public with good visitor facilities.

After leaving Worksop, our train passes over the A57 Liverpool–Skegness trunk road at Manton Colliery, with its sidings access leading off in a backwards direction on our right. We make our way through flat but very green fields to Retford, passing the site of Ranby Halt, long since closed, immediately prior to running under the Great North Road, and on to Retford, over two sets of level crossings at Babworth, with its historic links with the Pilgrim Fathers.

Our line curves downwards to the right, by means of the underpass, to Retford's low level station, the entire structure being opened in the summer of 1966 in order to dispense with the necessity of literally crossing over the East Coast Main Line. If our train is one of those which terminate at Retford, it usually runs into platform 2 of the high level station, which is reached by continuing on a single track from Whisker Hill Junction, and round a series of tortuous curves to the main station.

To the northeast of the station is the centre of East Retford (to give it its proper name), whose focal point is a spacious, pedestrianised market square and the beautiful church of St. Swithins. Historic inns remind us of the town's prosperity during coaching days on the Great North Road; while the Chesterfield Canal makes its way through the town in interesting fashion, including an aqueduct and embankment over the valley of the River Idle. Retford's importance for travellers was increased by the opening of the Great Northern Railway in 1849 and the establishment of two depots for a large number of steam locomotives. These have now gone, but Retford remains a calling point for High Speed Trains on the East Coast Main Line, with some nine in each direction per day.

CITY OF DERBY
by Simon Hartropp

Now that Derby is an open station, here is a 1 hour alternative to watching other people's trains come and go while you wait for yours.

Turn right out of the station into Station Approach. Pause to look behind you at the Midland Railway crest. How many town and city badges can you recognize? Around your are reminders of the years when 'the railway' provided work, rest and play for its employees. B.R. Staff Association now runs the imposing institute, a building with facilities for the whole range of social and educational facilities. At the end of the car park is a feature of the old Derby station – the clock with the Midland Railway crest.

Past the Institute, an entire hamlet of Midland Railway Cottages have been restored by the Derbyshire Historic Buildings Trust. The soundness of the basic structures was a tribute to the original builders – but the plasterwork left a lot to be desired!

At the end of the main row is the inevitable public house, but its name and the 'Canal St' nameplate give clues to an earlier transport interchange. The Derby Canal gave access to the national waterway network via the Trent & Mersey Canal. Most of it has been filled in, but if you take the footpath off to the right (signposted Recreation Ground), a new metal footbridge crosses over one of the old cuts. This one was left to provide essential drainage – nowadays it runs directly into the River Derwent. Bass was one of those nineteenth century benevolent dignitaries who took an interest not only in his business but also civic affairs. His statue stands outside the Derby Museum. Today this green park is the venue for travelling fairs.

Continue towards the city centre over the undulating ground until you reach the large Cockpit Roundabout. Site of a very ancient sport (happily now banned), and the old Derby Ice Factory (vital in the days before fridges were available), it carries the inner Ring Road traffic away from the shopping district. Turn left along (lower) Traffic St, following the signposts for Loughborough (A6). Look across the dual carriageway to view the Derby Playhouse complex, and the Eagle Centre (If you have time, and want to look around there is a pedestrian underpass into the Eagle Centre). Continue along Traffic St until you reach London Road. If it's spring time look straight ahead up the hill to admire the display of naturalised bulb flowers in the verge. Turn left into London Rd. Set back behind traditional iron railings are the

Liversage Almshouses. Even though there is no vehicular access, they continue to be popular as they are well-maintained by the Liversage Charity. You can't just apply; prospective residents must be recommended to the Trustees.

Continue past the modern-fronted Queens Hall Methodist Mission until you reach the traffic lights. Turn left into Midland Rd, the new, automated General Post Office. Derby is a major mail centre for eight Travelling Post Offices pass through Derby Rail Station each night, and the East Midlands Airport, only 11 miles away, is the hub of first class airmail services in the U.K.

Near the station is the War Memorial, let into the wall of the Midland Hotel. If you are thinking of a week's holiday, perhaps using one of the B.R. Railtourer tickets (Midlands, East Midlands, North Midlands) then call in at the clutch of hotels opposite the station for tariffs – any one would make a good base.

MANSFIELD AND SHERWOOD FOREST

by Malcolm Goodall

'Near this stone grew a tree reputed to be the centre of the Ancient Forest of Shirewood,' states the inscription on a stone in Westgate, Mansfield, near the junction with St. John Street.

Mansfield today is a thriving community of 58,000 people, Sherwood Forest an internationally famous tourist attraction and heavy coal trains trundle across the 15-arch viaduct high above the town centre – but it is more than 20 years since passenger trains last called at the station, although the bistro-style refreshments sold in the old booking hall today are a big improvement.

A service of fast 'Sprinter' trains from Nottingham via Langley Mill – or eventually perhaps via Hucknall with a short piece of new construction at Robin Hood's Hills – would greatly improve public transport to Mansfield and Sherwood Forest – the remains of which are mainly to the east of the town.

For the present, Mansfield has a bus service from Alfreton & Mansfield Parkway station; a twice daily bus to Doncaster station; and an hourly bus from Newark Northgate and Castle stations – the last of these providing connections with main line trains to and from King's Cross. The prettiest way is probably by the infrequent Mansfield District bus 27 from Newark bus station (Tel: 0623 23679 for timings) via Averham, Southwell and Kirklington.

Mansfield has a large shopping centre, including an open market (Monday, Thursday, Friday and Saturday), a mining museum, a Civic Theatre and Arts Centre, an indoor leisure centre, a triple screen cinema and good range of clubs, pubs and restaurants.

1985 saw the inauguration of the Robin Hood Way, a footpath that starts at Nottingham Castle and winds for over 80 circuitous miles through Sherwood to the Visitor Centre at Edwinstowe set amid relict woodland and stagshead oaks. You can also explore the remains of Sherwood Forest by bicycle from various railheads. Particularly recommended are Clumber Park (see page 55), Newstead Abbey (home of the Byron family) and the ruins of the 12th century Rufford Abbey. Buses run every day from Mansfield and Nottingham Victoria bus stations to Rufford and Edwinstowe. Robin Hood no longer waylays travellers, but the Sheriff of Nottingham is still alive and well!

NOTTINGHAM

by R. Hood

General Booth, Torvill and Dean, Raleigh, Players and Boots. Household names, all of them from the city that prides itself on being the Queen of the Midlands. Forget about other places. Buy your ticket, hop on the train and speed your way to Nottingham. This is the place to be, and has been ever since prehistoric man first made a snug home for himself on the sandstone cliffs above Narrow Marsh. That's how it came to be known as Tigcuocobaucc, which means houses of caves.

Later settlers sailed their craft up the Trent, couldn't pronounce this tongue-twister and changed it to the homestead of their leader, an Anglo-Saxon gentleman who rejoiced in the name of Snot (somehow the 'S' got lost for the city, but survives in the suburb of Sneinton).

There's always plenty to see and do. Ride round the centre on the free buses to get the feel of the place, then spend all day window shopping. Don't forget to search out some Colwick cheese, spread it thickly on bread and butter, douse liberally with vinegar and devour greedily. Grab a fistful of leaflets from the information office in Milton Street (closed Saturday afternoons and Sunday) and dive underground for a guided tour of the city caves, to see where it all started. Escape from this claustrophobia to one of the central parks. Take your seat at Trent Bridge and listen to the sound of willow on leather; or catch the bus to the broad expanse of Wollaton Park, stroll by the lake and admire the herds of deer. If it rains, dash inside the palatial Hall and marvel at the natural history exhibits. The insect section is particularly good, but if creepy-crawlies give you the heeby-jeebies then head across the stable yard to the Industrial Museum, with its steam engines, lace machinery and other contrivances that helped the city to prosperity.

Having acquired a taste for the past, head back to the town and drop in at the Brewhouse Yard to see household scenes of yesteryear, and a collection of weird and wonderful potions in the old chemist's shop. Don't forget to look round the spooky cellars. Climb up to the Castle grounds for the view; inside is the Fine Arts Museum. Just down Castle Road is one of the few remaining timber-framed buildings, saved in the nick of time and restored to house a dazzling display of Nottingham Lace. Next door, see how this was applied for adornment in the Costume Museum; then brave the traffic on Maid Marian Way to get to Canal Street and the Pickfords warehouse, its watery recesses telling the story of inland navigation. Exhausted by all this, recover in the 'Narrow Boat' which brews its own beer.

Wondering what to do in the evening? There are night clubs and discos, while the cosmopolitan population presents a varied international cuisine. Glide on to the ice rink, knock hell out of the tenpins in the bowling alley opposite, sail on Holme Pierreport Water Sports Centre, have a dip in the swimming baths – or, for a more leisurely pastime, wander through the lace market and marvel at the brickwork canyons created by eminent architects to house the lace trade. Queue for seats at the magnificent concert hall or hasten to the October Goose Fair. Then . . . but I've run out of space. Jump on the train to Nottingham and see for yourself. I'll meet you by the lions in Slab square!

FOR FURTHER INFORMATION

EAST MIDLANDS TOURIST BOARD, Exchequergate, Lincoln, LN2 1PZ covers most of the area of this guide, plus Lincolnshire. The Board publishes an annual guidebook, a leisure map and various specialist booklets. Bedfordshire, however, is covered by the THAMES & CHILTERNS TOURIST BOARD, 8 Market Place, Abingdon, Oxon. OX14 3UD.

MAPS: We recommend the Ordnance Survey maps, of various scales – for details write to Information and Public Enquiries, Ordnance Survey, Romsey Road, Maybush, Southampton, SO9 4DH. Also very useful are the National series published by John Bartholomew & Sons Ltd., Duncan Street, Edinburgh, EH9 1TA.

RAIL INFORMATION is obtainable from all staffed stations and British Rail appointed Travel Agents. Principal station information offices in the area covered by this book are:

Bedford 0234-60230	Milton Keynes 0908-70883
Derby 0332-32051	Northampton 0788-60116
Kettering 0536-521445	Nottingham 0602-476151
Leicester 0533-29811	Sheffield 0742-26411
London 01-387-7070	

British Rail publish a passenger timetable for the whole country, of over 1200 pages, issued twice a year, on sale at staffed stations and booksellers. Free timetable booklets and leaflets are also available for individual lines or groups of lines, as are leaflets on the carriage of bicycles by train, facilities for the disabled, railcards, rover tickets etc.

BUS INFORMATION: During 1986, a new Transport Act comes into effect, which could have far-reaching effects on bus services in this and other parts of England. You are therefore advised to check locally when planning journeys.

Principal bus companies in the East and North Midlands are:

Barton Transport plc, High Road, Chilwell, Nottingham, NG9 4AD (Tel: 254881).

Chesterfield Borough Transport, Stonegravels Depot, Sheffield Rd., Chesterfield, Derbyshire, S41 7JW (Tel: 76666).

City of Nottingham Transport, Lower Parliament Street, Nottingham, NG1 1GG (Tel: 504665).

Derby City Transport, Ascot Drive, London Rd., Derby, DE2 8ND (Tel: 31111).

East Midland Motor Services Ltd. (Mansfield), New Street, Chesterfield, Derbyshire, S40 2LQ (Tel: 77451).

Leicester City Transport, Abbey Park Rd., Leicester, LE4 5AH (Tel: 24326).

Midland Fox Ltd., Keswick House, 30 Peacock Lane, Leicester, LE1 5NY (Tel: 29161).

Northampton Borough Transport, St. James, Northampton, NN1 1GS (Tel: 51431).

Trent Motor Traction Co. Ltd., PO Box 35, Uttoxeter New Rd., Derby, DE3 3NJ (Tel: 372078).

United Counties Omnibus Co. Ltd., Bedford Rd., Northampton, NN1 5NN (Tel: 35661).

COME AND JOIN US!

The Railway Development Society is a national, voluntary, independent body which campaigns for better rail services, for both passengers and freights, and greater use of rail transport.

It publishes books and papers, holds meetings and exhibition, sometimes runs special trains and generally endeavours to put the case for rail to politicians, civil servants, commerce and industry and the public at large; as well as feeding users' comments and suggestions to British Rail management and unions.

Membership is open to all who are in general agreement with the aims of the Society and subscriptions (as at May 1986) are:

Standard rate: **£6**
Reduced rate: (for pensioners, full-time students) **£3**
Families: **£5** (plus £1 for each member of household)
Special rates also apply for corporate bodies.

Write to the Membership Secretary, Mr F. J. Hastilow, 21 Norfolk Road, Sutton Coldfield, West Midlands, B75 6SQ.

The **EAST MIDLANDS BRANCH** of the Society covers Leicestershire, Northhamptonshire and most of Bedfordshire. Its secretary is Mr. G. Moran, 89 Pipers Hill Road, Kettering, Northants, NN15 7NN.

The **NORTH MIDLANDS BRANCH** covers Nottinghamshire and Derbyshire. Its secretary is Mr R. M. Goodall, Albemarle Cottage, Kirklington Rd., Eakring, Nottingham, NG22 0DA.

There are many local rail users' groups, the majority of whom are affiliated to the Railway Development Society. Those in the area covered by this book include:

Bedford Commuters' Association. R. M. S. Lincoln, 9 Huntsman Way, Milton Ernest, Bedford, MK44 1SA.
Bedford-Bletchley Rail Users' Association. Chairman: Richard Crane, 23 Hatfield Crescent, Bradford, MK41 9RA.
Wellingborough Rail Users' Association. Chairman: Mrs. Pat Conway, 3 Oakwood Road, Northampton.
Kettering Rail Users' Association. Christopher Groome, 22 Duke Street, Burton Latimer, Kettering, NN15 5SG.
Corbyrail. Elisabeth Jordan, 13 Arnhill Rd., Gretton, Corby, NN17 3DN.
Melton-Oakham-Stamford Travellers' Assn. Darryl Taylor-Smith, 4 Lindon Avenue, Countesthorpe, Leicester, LE8 3PG.
Attenborough Rail Users' Association. Mrs. J. J. Copping, 33 Allendale Avenue, Attenborough, Notts.
Matlock-Sinfin Rail Users' Group. Simon Hartropp, 72 Empress Rd., Derby, DE3 6TE.
Lincoln-Newark-Nottingham Rail Users' Group. Basil Hewis, The Wharf, Trent Lane, Collingham, Newark, NG23 7LZ.
Hope Valley Rail Users' Group. Dr Hugh Porteous, 115 Wollaton Rd., Sheffield.
Peak Railway Society Ltd. Membership Secretary: Colin Peskett, 10 The Ridge, Sandygate, Sheffield, S10 4LL.